MOUNT BATTEN: FLYING BOAT BASE PLYMOUTH 1913 — 1986

Dennis C. Teague

Sunderland Flying Boat on Patrol
1940: One of the aircraft for which the Station was to become world famous, the *Short Sunderland* flying boat. This particular aircraft, N9048 RB-A, was the first machine flown by No. 10 Squadron Royal Australian Air Force from R.A.F. Station Mount Batten and came to an untimely end when it was destroyed by bombing on the night of 28th November, 1940.

This version of the book is virtually as originally published, presenting the work of Dennis C Teague. There are now additional pages at the back providing information about the publisher, Arthur L Clamp.

The republishing project is being managed by Arthur's grandson, Steven Gibson. We aim to find all the research that he was involved in publishing, preserving it for the next generation as part of 'The Clamp Collection'.

CONTENTS

List of Station's Commanding Officers
Introduction
R.N.A.S. Station Cattewater, 1913-18
R.A.F. Station Cattewater, 1918-28
R.A.F. Station Mount Batten, 1928-39
The War Years, 1939-45
The Aussies
The Post-war Years
Helicopter Air Sea Rescue
Station Buildings and their Use
Then and Now Pictorial
The Southern Maritime Air Region
Appendix and Postscript
List of Illustrations

ROYAL AIR FORCE MOUNT BATTEN: COMMANDING OFFICERS

Date	Officer
15 Jan. 1929	Wg.Cdr. S.W. Smith, O.B.E.
1 Oct. 1931	Wg.Cdr. J.P. Burling, D.S.C., D.F.C., A.F.C.
31 Dec. 1932	Wg.Cdr. J.O. Andrews, D.S.O., M.C.
21 Feb. 1934	Gp.Capt. I.T. Lloyd
7 Jun. 1935	Wg.Cdr. J.A. Sadler
20 Jan. 1936	Gp.Capt. P.E. Maitland, M.V.O., A.F.C.
5 Feb. 1937	Wg.Cdr. K.B. Lloyd, A.F.C.
19 Oct. 1937	Gp.Capt. E. Digby Johnson, A.F.C.
15 Dec. 1939	Gp.Capt. H.W. Evans
8 Jan. 1942	Gp.Capt. L. Martin, A.F.C.
1 Apr. 1943	Gp.Capt. J. Alexander, O.B.E., R.A.A.F.
7 Nov. 1944	Gp.Capt. W.S. Caster, M.C.
1 Feb. 1946	Sqn.Ldr. W.M. Lloyd
1 Apr. 1961	Wg.Cdr. L.R. Flower, M.B.E., M.M.
23 Mar. 1964	Wg.Cdr. D.T. Beamish, O.B.E.
30 Sep. 1966	Wg.Cdr. E.N. Stone, M.B.E.
4 Apr. 1969	Wg.Cdr. P. Wevill
28 Sep. 1970	Wg.Cdr. K.P. Lucas
14 Aug. 1972	Wg.Cdr. J.N. Burgess
28 Aug. 1974	Wg.Cdr. A. Redfern
22 Oct. 1976	Wg.Cdr. J.E.F. Williams
9 Feb. 1979	Wg.Cdr. J.S. Fosh
23 Aug. 1982	Wg.Cdr. B.J. Main
28 Feb. 1986	Sqn.Ldr. D.G. Edwards

© Copyright Dennis C. Teague

Wing Commander B. Main, M.Mar. E.C.O., R.A.F., the last Marine Branch Commanding Officer.

As the last Marine Branch Station Commander at Royal Air Force, Mount Batten, it is a great privilege, indeed honour, to be invited to write a brief foreword to this history of the Station. The disbandment of the Marine Branch marks the end of an era and quite naturally to both present serving personnel and the many retired "mariners" it is also a very sad occasion. However, it is worth remembering that Mount Batten is not just about R.A.F. Marine Craft. Indeed, there has been a Royal Air Force presence at the Mount Batten site since 1st April 1918, initially as R.A.F. Cattewater and then after a brief break in the late 1920's as R.A.F. Mount Batten. It can be said that the history of the Royal Air Force at Mount Batten is as long as the history of the Service itself; the Station has been associated with both the sea and the air in a time of war since it opened as Royal Naval Air Station, Cattewater in 1917. I have read this history and found that in many ways it is a history of the maritime elements of the Royal Air Force.

My admiration goes out to the author and also all those people who have given of their time, knowledge, photographs and memories. To read such a book of R.A.F. Mount Batten is a pleasurable experience and after serving for three and a half years as a Station Commander I was not surprised to find that my efforts to dig into the history have done little more than scratch the surface. It is fascinating to read and see how the aircraft have changed over the years but the outward appearance of the Station has changed but little in all the time since 1918. Looking at the various photographs through the years it is also very reassuring both for the past, the present and very much for the future that although the aircraft, the tools and the uniforms have changed the all important element, that is our Service personnel, do not appear to have changed all that much.

As I said at the beginning it is a sad day to see the disbandment of a Branch and as I write this the future of the Station is very uncertain, no doubt there have been similar periods of uncertainty before but R.A.F. Mount Batten on such a superb site and with a long and honourable history has always survived. It is always difficult to pick out special points in a history but reading this book I feel that this is a history that everyone can be proud of and for all ex-Mount Batten personnel this book should help it remain a place of pleasant memories.

INTRODUCTION

During the preparation of the manuscript for my book about the Royal Australian Air Force Sunderland crews operating from Britain 1939—1945 it became evident that the bases from which they flew had long and interesting histories themselves. Pembroke Dock in Wales has been the subject of an excellent illustrated booklet by my friend John Evans entitled *Flying Boat Haven* ISBN 0 9510411 O.X which came out in 1985 and this is about Mount Batten whilst Poole has also appeared in print.

I was fortunate that Colin Lovelock an ex-Wing Commander, D.F.C., R.A.F., decided to visit Australia and he told many ex-crews of my books so they then sent me great piles of unpublished material for the *Sunderlanders* book and this one. Colin also helped me a lot as he had served at Mount Batten pre-War and later as the Commanding Officer of 461 Squadron R.A.A.F. for a period of time during the War and many of his unique photographs are included in this book.

It is interesting to include shots from unknown amateur photographers and I have had considerable help from very kind persons who have removed snaps from albums for my use; likewise information has come from many and diverse sources. This is in no way intended as an in depth or complete history as almost every week new items of interest come to light but more or less as a general guide spanning the years.

Today the Station still operates only as a shadow of it's former glory and as it ends it's life one has to wonder as to the wisdom of this and why commonsense no longer prevails. Britain is an island. Britain has many harbours from which flying boats could operate against their old enemy the submarine. Many share the view that the Falklands Campaign could have used amphibian aircraft for early warning radar aircraft. Runways then become far less important and bombing water doesn't have all that much effect.

The two Wars have done little to influence the "powers that be" that seaplanes and flying boats have an important place in today's defence system. The ostrich-type outlook prevails nearly everywhere except in Japan and Canada with the U.S. Coastguards still using amphibians. The Canadian CL 215 went into production as late as 1969 and today is in use as a water bomber against the forest fires but as an amphibian would be ideal for off-shore patrolling. Armed with torpedoes plus either missiles or depth bombs, the Japanese have three Squadrons of *Shin Meiwa* long range patrol flying boats and, like Britain, they are also an island race.

R.A.F. Mount Batten has had a long and distinguished career and one can only hope that this will continue in one form or another. At the time of writing, January 1986, various dates have been bandied about for a closure of the Station and the most recent suggestion for its usage has been a Royal Marine occupation but this seems unlikely; only time will tell and it would not surprise me to see it's life extended.

Credits: I would like to thank everyone who has contributed towards this publication but this is not possible as most of the photographs have come to me via collections and albums. However, others have been received from the Royal Australian Air Force, the Australian War Memorial Canberra, the Point Cook Museum and the Royal Air Force Museum. Others from Wing Commander V. Hodgkinson, D.F.C., R.A.A.F. Rtd., Sqdn.Ldr. P. Jensen, R.A.A.F. Rtd., Wing Commander R.K. Philips, R.A.A.F. Rtd., the late Wing Commander C. Lovelock, D.F.C., R.A.F. Rtd. I would also like to thank Wing Commanders Fosh and Main, both C.Os of the Station and Mr. T. Hugo for their assistance with special thanks to Mr. T.D. Jago, R.I.B.A. for his drawing. The Cornwall Aero Park at Helston who have a permanent display of photographs and recovered items from war-time Mount Batten in the R.A.A.F. exhibition, and C.A.S. Property Consultants, Stoke, Plymouth.

I would also like to thank Mrs. C. Lovelock, Mr. A. J. Cowell, and Mr. A. Clamp for the loan of photographs and Vic Fowler (Plymouth) Photography.

Dennis C. Teague, A.R.Ae.S.,
F.I.P.M., F.P.C.S.,
1, Fisher Road, Stoke,
Plymouth PL2 3BA
Devon

1 No. 1 Hangar
2 No. 2 Hangar
3 Workshops
4 Engine Test House
5 Workshops
6 Mt. Batten Pier
7 Sick Quarters
8 Castle Inn
9 Quarters
10 Station Offices
11 No. 3 Hangar
12 No. 4 Hangar
13 Slipway
14 Power House
15 Quarters
16 Met Office
17 Stone Jetty
18 The Tower

Royal Naval Air Service Station Cattewater 1913-18

The sheltered water known as the *Cattewater*, which had provided a haven for shipping, had been idle for many years. Since the Civil War little of note had taken place on the land now occupied by R.A.F. Mount Batten. However, in 1906 a firm called the *Plymouth Fish Guano and Oil Company* started up business in a building there converting dog fish (known also as Huss, Rock Salmon, etc.) into fertiliser, the fish market on Sutton Harbour providing the waste which was transported over to the factory. It can be imagined that in the summer, with the wind in the right direction, the resulting smell carried over Plymouth so in 1912 the factory was forced to close down for a while having had an injunction made against it. The landing of dogfish, however, was becoming big business and it was not until 1917 that the Royal Navy closed it down.

In 1913 seaplane trials were carried out, but it is not too clear by whom, except that the results interested the Royal Navy. Claude Graham-White is known to have given exhibition flights at Torquay round that time and in 1913 *The Daily Mail* organised their seaplane trial around Britain. A small site was allocated for aircraft and maintained during September of that year near the Fish Fertiliser factory! Plans for developing the site went ahead and by 1916 a Naval establishment was agreed which opened in 1917 complete with buildings although these were wooden construction and one suspects of a war-time temporary nature. The stone pier had a railway track laid on it so as to enable a steam crane to run along and hoist seaplanes out of the water up on to it. Hangars were constructed and R.N.A.S. Cattewater went operational with *Short* 184 seaplanes which were quite large machines, these fourteen were joined by a *Large America* flying boat, seven *Hamble Baby* and two *Sopwith Baby* machines. Patrols were undertaken in coastal waters in conjunction with the airships which operated from Laira nearby and the main base at Mullion on the Lizard in Cornwall.

The recommissioning ceremony in 1918 in front of the former *Castle Inn* and H.M.S. *Rapid* ferrying personnel to R.N.A.S. *Cattewater* from the Barbican.

Early Photographs
1914-1918: Not a great deal is known about the wartime days at R.N.A.S. Cattewater but a large number of service personnel were stationed on the base. The *Short* 184 aircraft were the mainstay being maintained in the hangar and stored on the stone jetty. Off duty, either the ferryboats to Plymouth or the "on station" Inn provided relaxation. Photograph of the Officers' Mess.

Short 184s on the Breakwater

Short 184s on the stone jetty: The method of transferring the seaplanes from the storage areas was by the steam crane which hoisted them either in or out of the sea. Although these aircraft may look small on the jetty the wing span was some 63 feet which accounted for the length of the jib of the crane

Large America Flying Boat

Curtiss H Series known as *Large America*, this was designed by a Briton who emigrated to the U.S.A. and joined Curtiss aircraft makers. His America flying boat was very well received and the British Admiralty bought 64 mainly built in the U.K. The *Large America*, H8, H12 and H16 of which the R.N.A.S. had 75. One or two were based at R.N.A.S. Cattewater, others in the Isles of Scillies.

Royal Air Force Station Cattewater
1918-28

In 1918 when the R.N.A.S. was absorbed into the R.A.F. the Station became Royal Air Force Mount Batten until it went to Care and Maintenance before it was run down in 1922. During its short four-year period it came under No. 19 Group S.W. Area and No. 10 Coastal Defence Force; five Flights were formed until these were redesignated Squadrons. Flts. 347, 348 and 349 became 237 Squadron; 420, 421, 422 and 423 became 238 Squadron. 237 operated *Short* 184 and 240s, 238 had *Short* 240, *Felixstowe* F2A, F3, F5s also two *Sopwith Baby* seaplanes.

Cattewater Seaplane Depot was gradually run down. However, the arrival of the NC 4 American flying boat on 31st May, 1919, made it world famous when the first trans-Atlantic crossing via Newfoundland and the Azores had been made. May, 1919, saw No. 237 Squadron disband and in April, No. 238 followed likewise and the end looked in sight.

The wartime events of the Station's aircraft are very hard to find recorded but it is known that the *Short* 184s did operate patrols in the area of the Eddystone lighthouse and local knowledge states that an enemy submarine was attacked but it is difficult to confirm this. The R.N.A.S. airships from Laira, Plymouth, and Mullion, near Helston, are known to have played an important role in anti-submarine work during this period but it would appear that like those who followed them during World War Two the flying boats undertook the same monotonous work with little to show for all their hardships.

Cattewater had several interesting aspects during it's career not the least being home to the largest number of Women's Royal Naval Service or W.R.N.S. (Wrens) as they were better known. The girls earned the respect of even the most chauvinistic of the men. It also was the beginning of what was to be one of the longest running bases and the four hangars, although only three now exist, have been recladded and refurbished, originated from the 1917—1918 structures. February, 1917, saw the base opened and the existing buildings cleared to make way for huts which remained until 1938, the *Castle Inn* becoming the first *Greenleaf House* residence of the Station Commander.

In 1923 a Bill had been presented in Parliament entitled *The Cattewater Seaplane Station Bill* and received its final reading thus enabling the Air Ministry to purchase the land and develop the site as an R.A.F. base. Over the next five years the building work changed the face of the old base; quarters were provided for flying and ground staffs together with ample hangarage for the aircraft of the time. The main two were on the sheltered side of the base facing the north and away from the prevailing south-westerly winds, shielded by the large rocky centre of the site.

Maintenance Work at R.A.F. Cattewater
A nice shot of the mighty *Short* 184 coastal patrol aircraft, note the bombs under the centre section. An enemy U boat was sunk by one of these aircraft. No. 237 Marine Operations Squadron of the R.A.F. operated these seaplanes from August, 1918, until it was disbanded in May, 1919. R.A.F. Cattewater continued operating until 1922.

First Transatlantic Flight, 1919

NC 4: A fine view of the *Curtis* NC 4 flying boat which had made the first aerial crossing of the Atlantic, 16th to 31st May, 1919. Three aircraft had commenced on the 1st May, the first leg of the trip from Rockaway New York to Newfoundland. After several stops they arrived on the 12th to depart on the 16th. Two aircraft had to force land enroute; one crew was rescued and the other flying boat made it to port on the sea. No. 4 flew on to the Azores and Lisbon reaching Mount Batten with a R.A.F. escort. Note in the lower photograph the British *Felixstowe* F2A, N4449, flying boat in the background.

Royal Air Force Station Mount Batten
1st October, 1928

The requirement for a base which could provide coverage of the Western Approaches to Britain had been realised from the experience learned in the 1914—18 War and this was one of the prime reasons for the new Station. It was, in fact, designated as part of the defence of South-West England. For this reason in early 1929 it went operational when in January, No. 203 Squadron was formed from No. 482 Coastal Reconnaissance Flight and equipped with *Supermarine Southamptons* a relatively new machine which had entered service in 1925. This twin-engined biplane flying boat was to see service for quite a long time with Coastal Command. 203 took them to Iraq when they departed in April, 1929, and retained them until 1935 replacing with the *Scapa* made by the same firm and an improved version in most ways to the *Southampton* Mk X. In February, 1929, another Squadron was formed being 204 and equipped with the *Fairey* IIID seaplanes until they converted over to *Southamptons*.

The next squadron to reform was No. 209. On the 15th January, 1930, they came into being with the large *Blackburn Iris* flying boats. Only three were produced and these were replaced by the *Blackburn Perths* but not before one had come to grief. 209 departed on the 1st May, 1935.

In July, 1930, three *Southamptons* departed for the Icelandic Parliament celebrations with the intention of setting up the longest formation flight but although one of the aircraft completed the trip a second had to put down in the Faroes when the pilot was taken ill and the third developed engine trouble but completed the rest of the journey later. In March of this year two of 209 Squadron's aircraft had made the first East to West direct crossing of the Merditerranean. Another record for the Station was made in 1931 when Gibraltar to Britain non-stop flight was completed. For a while the Station was without its flying boats when 204 left for a tour of duty in the Suez Canal zone with their new *Saro Londons* and a change of type and command took place when two Royal Naval Fleet Air Arm units arrived with single-engined seaplanes. No. 407 Fleet Fighter Unit flew *Hawker Osprey* biplanes and No. 444 Fleet Spotter Reconnaissance Flight had *Fairey* IIIFs.

The visiting aircraft carriers fitted their machines with floats and these also used the base and an unusual machine being a *Wapiti* fitted with floats. An aircraft, en route to Singapore, set up another long distance journey when on the 23rd July, 1935, a *Short Singapore* II, K4581, on a delivery flight to join 205 Squadron, made the trip with twelve staged set downs.

No account of the Station would be complete without mention of "Aircraftsman Shaw" who was, in fact, Colonel T.E. Lawrence known better as "Lawrence of Arabia" who served during the 1930s at Mount Batten. A lot has been written about his career and possibly the latter years in the R.A.F. have been left as they would provide too much contrast to his earlier years. Those that knew him have mixed feelings. However, all tend to agree that he played a large part in the advancement of the High Speed Air Sea Rescue launches and that he was involved in the rescue of the crew of one of 209 Squadron's *Blackburn Iris* flying boats which crashed in Plymouth Sound killing most of the crew. He spent some time working on the development of the pinnace with the makers of the first two trial boats and brought one of them back to Plymouth.

The design by Hubert Scott-Paine of a new hull format with a "V" shape instead of the conventional round hull, altered the concept of high-speed boats. The Air Ministry was interested in the 37½ foot vessel and Lawrence with Cpl. Bradbury were involved with the trials. It is said that he foresaw the use of vessels for high-speed rescue work rather than as tenders which at the time was the official use and that he influenced the 40 foot and the well known 64 foot H.S.Ls. T.E. Lawrence spent from 1930 to 1933 at the base.

He was, at the time of his death in a motorcycle accident, still serving with the R.A.F. under the assumed name of "Aircraftsman Shaw" and with his passing a colourful character was lost. A view widely held at the time was that he transferred to the Air Force to avoid threats on his life yet other views were he wanted peace and quiet. Whatever was the truth he enjoyed a privileged existence unlike many other aircraftsmen.

In August, 1936, No. 204 Squadron returned and the following year, after visits to Malta and Gibraltar four of the Squadron's *Saro Londons* Mk IIs, fitted with long-range fuel tanks, took part in a round trip to Australia taking with them Air Commodore Goble of the Royal Australian Air Force. The flying boats concerned were K5911, K5913, K6929, K6930 and K6927, the latter had quite an eventful trip shedding a propellor over the Bay of Bengal on the 16th December and having to force land. It was towed to Akyab by the SS *Jalagopal* and repaired by an engineer officer who was flown from Singapore. On the return flight to Britain K6927 was in trouble again and had to put down near Rangoon and had a second tow. The flight to Darwin in Australia had taken to the 17th January, 1938, and when the 204 Squadron's aircraft returned they had flown over 30,000 miles and more than 400 flying hours.

The Station during the 1930s put on for the public *Open Days* and *Empire Day* air shows which attracted large numbers from all around the area. In those days a steam ferry plied its way from Plymouth's famous area, the Barbican, where the Pilgrim Fathers and Sir Francis Drake many years before had sailed. On these public days this service had to be enhanced and augmented with the other boats which normally took visitors on tours of the Dockyard and Warships. The Station, although space was at a premium, put on every kind of display that they could ranging from fire fighting to fly pasts by the latest aircraft. Only days after the new *Hurricane* fighter had set a record speed from London to Scotland, it appeared and flew around at an Air Show as did the latest flying boat the *Sunderland* on another occasion. Very few people watching could have even dreamed what a part this aircraft was to play in the future of the base in later years. It circled and overflew showing the superb shape contrasting so markedly with the biplane flying boats based there. One was allowed to climb into some of the seaplanes such as the *Swordfish* of No. 821 Squadron and the *Blackburn Sharks* of No. 2 Anti-Aircraft Co-operation Unit plus a walk round the impressive *Stranraer*, *Singapore* III visitors and the *Londons*.

The forthcoming war in Europe was to be reflected in the nature of the display items as the 1930s ran out. The fire-fighting displays were replaced by men in gas protective clothing; defences were shown with sand-bagged emplacements and generally an air of expectancy prevailed.

Looking back to those days, a dignified optimism that this serene atmosphere would last for ever seemed to be echoed in the neat, tidy, orderly layout of the Station; the new Officers' Mess was built overlooking the Sound and surrounded with pleasant green areas. Tennis courts, boating, fishing and other sports provided relaxing off-duty periods. The large silver machines were kept spotless as were the buildings which housed the equipment, stores and workshops. A tidy Station in every aspect. The typical pre-War attitudes abounded with "rank all important" yet the servicemen, at all levels, enjoyed life and only thought that a war in Europe would be more of a nuisance than a threat. Britain's Navy was supreme and not, like the 1914—18 War, the aircraft of the R.A.F., were not only equal but in many cases superior to other nations. It appeared that like the last time most of the fighting would take place between the two rows of fortifications so what did Mount Batten have to worry about? In any case six months should see it over.

This view fortunately was not shared by the higher levels of Command and the memories of the U boat warfare still remained together with the realisation that the Western Approaches were the lifeline and the enemy U boat fleet was growing. New aerodromes were built in Cornwall and Devon to provide aerial coverage of the supply convoy routes in case the enemy submarines were let loose to harrass the merchant fleets. St. Eval near Newquay, Portreath and Perranporth along the same coast towards Lands End, Predannack on the Lizard and Davidstow Moor were built in Cornwall. St. Mawgan developed for incoming aircraft from the U.S.A. In Devon Chivenor near Barnstaple, Dunkeswell built for the R.A.F. and passed over to the U.S. Navy, Harrowbeer near Plymouth, Winkleigh and Bolt Head were constructed whilst Exeter was improved.

The principal flying boat bases in the area were Mount Batten and Pembroke Dock, in Wales, and although many of the above were not actually commenced until after the outbreak of War, the land had been either purchased or was in the negotiating stage. Britain was more prepared than is generally realised. The actual strength of the Squadrons of aircraft allocated to Coastal Command, however, fell far short of what was required. The *Avro Anson* was the mainstay and whilst a fine machine, it did not measure up to the opposition and soon was replaced. The flying boat scene was completely different. The *Sunderland* entered service just before War was declared and served with great distinction throughout the hostilities and well into the post-War years and even into another War when it operated in Korea.

Mount Batten's Squadrons comprised of No. 209 with *Stranraers* which had arrived in December, 1938, and they departed a year later in December, 1939. No. 204 had taken *Sunderlands* on charge and converted over to them at Plymouth being based from June, 1939, to April, 1940, while two more R.A.F. *Sunderland* Squadrons were based at Pembroke Dock being No. 228 and No. 210 whilst the first squadron to be formed, No. 230, were overseas when War was declared.

Collision with Dockyard Tug

The tail of an *Iris* flying boat stands above the water line, the plane having hit the steam pinnace, *Alexanda*, after alighting on Plymouth Sound in 1933.

Group of Officers

No. 204 Squadron in the early 1930s, probably 1931 prior to the Squadron departing for a tour of duty in the Suez canal zone. The Squadron had returned by the end of the decade and were on station at the outbreak of war with their *Sunderlands*.

Officers, Sergeants and Corporals of No. 209 Squadron

This Squadron was formed in January, 1930, Flying Boat Squadron and was equipped with Blackburn Iris Flying Boats and later Perth Flying Boats. These two rare photographs show its officers and some of the other ranks presumably at the time of the Squadron's formation. The officers are P/Sgt. Saffery, F/O Baines, F/O Bonsey, F/O Goodhart, P/O Jenkins (back row) and F/O Rees, Flt. Lt. Chilton, Sqn. Ldr. Jones, F/O Gurney, F/O Brown (front row).

Hawker Osprey II seaplane (upper photograph) 1935

An interesting photograph showing an *Osprey* off one of the slipways at Mount Batten during 1932-1936. The flying boats had moved away to the Suez Canal Zone in the Middle East, apart from the few from visiting Squadrons, and for a while the Royal Navy Nos. 407 and 444 Fleet Fighter Flights took up residence. They had a mixture of aircraft, No. 407 with *Ospreys* formed the 2nd Cruiser Squadron's Catapult Squadron up to mid-1936. No. 444 was the Catapult Squadron for the 1st Catapult Squadron and flew *Shark*, *Osprey*, *Swordfish* and *Walrus* planes.

Westland Wapiti IIa J9498 (lower photograph)

This is one of probably three *Wapiti* aircraft converted to a floatplane for trials and was attached to No. 444 Fleet Fighter Flight in the early 1930s. Little is known as to the outcome of these trials but *Wapitis* continued to serve with the R.A.F. in various parts of the world in other roles such as Army Co-operation and reconnaissance work.

Supermarine Southampton Flying Boat

This 1929 photograph shows a Southampton Mk. 1, S1301, taxiing to its mooring in the Cattewater with the old pier in view in the background. This flying boat belonged to 203 Squadron which was formed at Mount Batten in 1929.

Blackburn Iris Flying Boat

Maintenance work is taking place on this flying boat in one of the large hangars at Mount Batten sometime in 1930. No. 209 Squadron was equipped with three of these Iris which were in use with the Squadron until 1934 when they were replaced with the more powerful Perth flying boats fitted with three 825 h.p. Buzzard engines.

Supermarine Southampton Flying Boats

A graceful descent to Plymouth Sound appears to be taking place with these planes over the crowded townscape of pre-war Plymouth. They were with No. 203 Squadron and came to Mount Batten in 1929 then shortly transferred for service to Iraq until 1939. These were the first of the large seaplanes to be deployed at Mount Batten and heralded in for the station a new era of service. The Southampton flying boats were replaced with Blackburn Iris flying boats. The sad remains of part of the framework of a Southampton flying boat was photographed in a scrapyard sometime in 1954. It is unfortunate that in spite of the many kinds of flying boats built very few are preserved in museums throughout the world today.

Fairey IIID Seaplane

A very good view of this seaplane with its two large sea floats is afforded by this photograph of it out of water. These seaplanes were attached to No. 204 Squadron which was formed on 1st February, 1929, the year of this picture. The Squadron remained at Mount Batten until April, 1940.

Scapa Flying Boat

This was fitted with Rolls Royce engines and became operational with No. 204 Squadron during the early 1930s although this particular photograph is dated 1936 and shows the seaplane visiting Calshot. Like other flyingboats of a similar size, they were a familiar sight in the Mount Batten locality for some years.

Short Singapore III Flying Boat

These were attached to No. 209 Squadron at Mount Batten and were engaged on anti-piracy patrols during 1937 linked with the Spanish Civil War. The upper photograph shows one taxiing across Plymouth Sound and in the lower and much closer view of another practice bombs are being fitted to the underside of the lower wing by station personnel.

Mount Batten to Australia 1937

The following selection of photographs shows several of the aircraft which were involved in a historic flight from Mount Batten to Australia by No. 204 Squadron. *Saro Londons* were used, K5911, K5913, K6927 and K6929. Colin Lovelock was the pilot of K6927 and kindly donated these photographs. The one showing K5911 clearly shows the large long-range fuel tank situated behind the cockpit. Of note in the pictures of the refuelling are the laborious method of rolling the drums of fuel along the jetty for hand pumping into the tanks. The two crew members are Pilot Officer Hyde to the left and Pilot Officer Lovelock. Note the front gun ring.

R.A.F. MOUNT BATTEN 1939-45

No. 204 Squadron had six machines when War was declared on 3rd September, 1939, and almost at once their aircraft became operational flying out over the seas to the south-west of Britain. Only fourteen days after the War had commenced the first official action was recorded by the Sunderlands from Mount Batten. Reference has been made to a sighting on the 9th but there is nothing to confirm this and it probably was one of the large number of false alarms in those early days.

There was, however, nothing false about the distress calls from the SS *Kensington Court* which had been torpedoed about 70 miles from the Isles of Scilly. One Sunderland was diverted to attack the submarine but on arrival found that the enemy had submerged so the area was bombed where it was likely to have been and then landed to take on fourteen survivors. Flt.Lt. Barrett of 204 Sq. in RF-E, L5802 was joined by another Sunderland from Pembroke Dock and 228 Squadron which took on twenty-one more and made her way back to Mount Batten. Later on in November Flt.Lt. Barrett received the D.F.C. medal.

All through the winter of 1939 No. 204 patrolled and provided air cover for the convoys losing one aircraft which crashed in Plymouth Sound at night, N9030. The crews expressed utter disgust at the lack of action little knowing that plans were being made to send them up North and replace them with the Australians working at Pembroke Dock. No. 204 departed and within days N9046 was to become famous when it fended off six Ju 88s twin-engined fighters and downed two of these. Soon the squadron was off again this time to West Africa where it served with distinction. R.A.F. Mount Batten was all set to become one of the most famous bases in the World.

Administration Changes 1940

The Station assumed administration control of nearby Roborough airfield and the Air Sea Rescue marine units No. 39 at Torquay, No. 41 at Salcombe and No. 43 at Fowey in mid-1940. Later in June No. 964/934 Squadron was formed on the stone jetty with barrage balloons for the defence of the city and also maintained the balloons that the ships carried. On the 1st July the No. 1 Air Despatch and Receipt Unit came into being.

R.A.F. Roborough is today the site of the city Airport but in those days was only a small historic patch of grass which had commenced back in the late 1920s and by 1931 had the same hangar which exists today. On the far side of the airfield the *George* public house also remains and it was in this pub and in buildings erected on the tennis courts that the crews of the biplane *Gloster Gladiators* of 247F Squadron operated and gained for the airfield the distinction of being the only operational biplane fighters of the R.A.F. to see service operationally during the Battle of Britain period. No. 19 Group Coast Command Communication Flight was established there and was to remain for another twenty or so years. The School of Navigation lasted for a year or so and so did No. 1623 Anti-Aircraft Flight which co-operated with the local AA gun batteries, this unit became 691 Squadron.

The Air Despatch and Receipt resulted from the successful flights of the Near East which the Station's aircraft had undertaken. Air cover for these flights was provided by *Blenheim* fighters from St. Eval which flew out as far as possible over the Bay of Biscay.

August saw a detachment of No. 10, four Sunderlands, being sent to Oban in Scotland for a short period and losing one aircraft during a night-flying accident. One of the British Overseas Air Corporations Short 'C' flying boats which were very similar to the Sunderland and had pioneered flying boat civil flying before the War, made several calls into Mount Batten during the period in 1940-42 when G-AFCZ *Clare* was lost off West Africa.

September saw Sqdn.Ldr. Garing taking part in the well publicised rescue of children being evacuated to Canada when their ship was torpedoed. V.I.P.s were flown out on the 12th when the Secretary of State for Air left and on the 17th the Commander in Chief Far East. On the 17th up in Scotland one of the detachment aircraft picked up twenty-one survivors of the S.S. *Stangrant* whilst at home an attack was made on a U boat without results. This story was to be repeated during November and December.

The night of November 27/28th, 1940, saw a heavy raid on the Station and the nearby oil tanks during which a hangar was destroyed containing Sunderland N9048 another at the moorings, P9601, and considerable damage done to the oil installations which burnt for several days.

A little known flight had taken place on the 18th June when a *Walrus* was flown from Roborough to Mount Batten en route to Brittany, France, on a clandestine mission to collect the wife and children of the Free French leader General de Gaulle. The crew comprised of two Australians, Flt.Lt. J. Napier Bell and Sgt. Harris with Cpl. Nowell of the R.A.F. They took off at 0255 hours and nothing more was heard of them; later it was discovered that the locals had heard the aircraft trying to land in foggy conditions and finally crash near Keranou with no survivors.

The unmistakable tower of Mount Batten which looks set to outlast the rock on which it stands.

A Sunderland Mk 1 of 204 Squadron R.A.F. It was this Squadron which Mount Batten went to war with and it remained until replaced by the Australians of No. 10 Squadron Royal Australian Air Force. Note the early wartime camouflage of green and earth brown on the sides and upper surfaces with sky undersides; also the well-known upper mid-turret has not yet been introduced and two beam-gun positions provide cover.

During the troubled days of 1940 great numbers of French troops were brought from France and this rare photograph shows numbers of them at Mount Batten with *Sunderland* RB-E of No. 10 Squadron R.A.A.F. moving out for take off.

This snap shot of Flt Lt Colin Lovelock, later Wing Commander with the D.F.C., and his crew on top of their Sunderland is interesting from the historical point of view as it shows the early exhaust pipes and non spinner propellors. The crew was normally of eleven although nine were common, all the crew were trained to be able to replace any other position in the flyingboat.

THE ROYAL AUSTRALIAN AIR FORCE 1940-45

It was one of those queer quirks of fate which had brought members of the R.A.A.F. to Britain to collect some of the new *Short Sunderland* flying boats and fly them home only to find that due to production delays both they and their aircraft would be here when war broke out. The pilots were being trained on R.A.F. aircraft at Pembroke Dock until their aircraft were ready. By October they were ready to fly out when they received the order to remain and that other members of the R.A.A.F. were on their way to join them. Throughout the winter of 1939 they worked up a new Squadron which was designated No. 10 and went operational in February, 1940. The set-up of the R.A.F. which had 3 Squadrons of eight machines making up 24 in all were re-organised into 4 Squadrons of six to include No. 10. No. 204 as we have seen went North from Mount Batten and was replaced by No. 10 which went operational right away.

Britain was, at that time, relatively safe and although the U boats had claimed victims around the coasts they themselves had to run the gauntlet from their bases in Germany either via the North Sea or the Channel and Coastal Command could patrol without fear from enemy fighter cover. This all changed with the fall of France and the enemy now occuped the U boat bases and airfields. The submarines could now operate from a coast line without having to return to the German shipyards and utilised the French ports. Just as serious was the fact that the long-range FW200s anti-shipping bombers took up residence accompanied by the hard-hitting JU88s and almost before one could realise it the Sunderlands and their convoys were no longer the hunters but the hunted. Enemy bombers attacked the Station in 1940, and the tide had turned in the enemy's favour.

The new R.A.A.F. Squadron had an eventful start to their operational career. Only a few weeks after they had settled down and worked up to an operational unit at a new base with sightings during May and June, the C.O., Flt.Lt. Pearce, on the 17th June sighted a submarine and dropped six bombs. No damage was claimed nor reported although this incident was later written up as a sinking. One of the Squadron's tasks was to fly V.I.Ps to various parts of the world and the next day 18th June, a flight was made to the French Government H.Q. at Bordeaux and another on the 19th. The 25th saw a flight to Rabat to try and obtain French co-operation in that area.

It was on the 1st July that the Australians scored their first success when together Flt.Lt. Gibson and H.M.S. *Gladiolus*, they shared half each the sinking of the U26. The U boat had attacked a convoy at night and had been attacked by the naval vessel causing it to run on the surface. In the morning it was sighted by H.M.S. *Rochester* and the No. 10 Squadron Sunderland. The ship opened fire and the aircraft dropped bombs causing the enemy to scuttle shortly afterwards. At home the bombing mentioned was in the shape of a Ju 88 dropping a stick of bombs without serious damage, a foretaste of what was to come in November. Photographic reconnaissance flights took place over St. Nazaire and Bordeaux on the 12th and 13th, on the latter day Flt.Lt. Gibson being attacked by fighters. An unusual event on the 14th was the 30 ton flying boat playing fighter and destroying one *Heinkel* III and routing others attacking a ship, F.O. Birch being the pilot. On the 28th Flt.Lt. Garing was escorting a ship when he was attacked on four occasions by Ju 88s and managed to drive them off.

THE BLITZ ON PLYMOUTH 1941

This will be best remembered as the year of the blitz on Plymouth which all but destroyed it. During the two months of March and April over 2000 Service and civilians were killed and three times as many badly injured. 3754 houses were totally destroyed with many others very badly damaged. Numbers do vary a lot and totals have been estimated as: 20th-21st March 20,000 buildings hit plus, 21st-23rd April and 28th-29th around 18,000 more making a total of 38,000 of which at least 18,000 and possibly as many as 19,000 were seriously damaged.

As a result of these attacks No. 10 Squadron was withdrawn to Pembroke Dock in Wales from 28th May to 31st December and the R.A.F. returned with flights to the Middle East. *Catalinas* and a few of the interesting *Short* 'G' Class flying boats of 119 Squadron also made a short appearance. These were pre-War designs and larger versions of the famous 'C' class for the North Atlantic routes. Fitted with turrets, three were tried out of which *Golden Fleece* sank on the 20th June. *Golden Hind* sprang a leak and together with *Golden Horn* was demobolised and returned to B.O.A.C. where they operated from Poole.

Anti-Aircraft Gun Position

It was very necessary to mount defensive guns in and around Mount Batten being situated very close to the heart of Plymouth and itself a target for attack. This amateur photograph shows the gun position built in front of the Officers' Mess in 1941.

Cold work in 1940: sweeping the snow off the wings

28th November, 1940

No. 10 Squadron hangar after enemy bombing the previous night. The burning oil tanks at Turnchapel, in the left background, and the remains of the station's headquarters and sergeants' sleeping quarters can be seen in the left foreground.

Damaged Sunderland

This was also part of the scene at the station after the raids during the night of 27th-28th November, 1940. The hangar and the plane, N9048, suffered considerable damage. This is the same aircraft shown in flight on page 1.

Damaged Airmen's Mess

This was part of the result of an attack on 15th July, 1940; the airmen's mess sustaining a direct hit while nearby buildings were damaged by blast and flying debris.

Plymouth Ablaze

John Smeaton's Eddystone lighthouse is silhouetted against the fires raging in the centre of Plymouth in March, 1941. This scene and the one below showing the movement of tracer bullets against the night sky was taken by an amateur Australian photographer.

Attack on Plymouth

The city was one of the most devastated centres of population in the country. The raids covered the years 1940 to 1944, thousands of buildings were destroyed and over 1,000 people were killed.

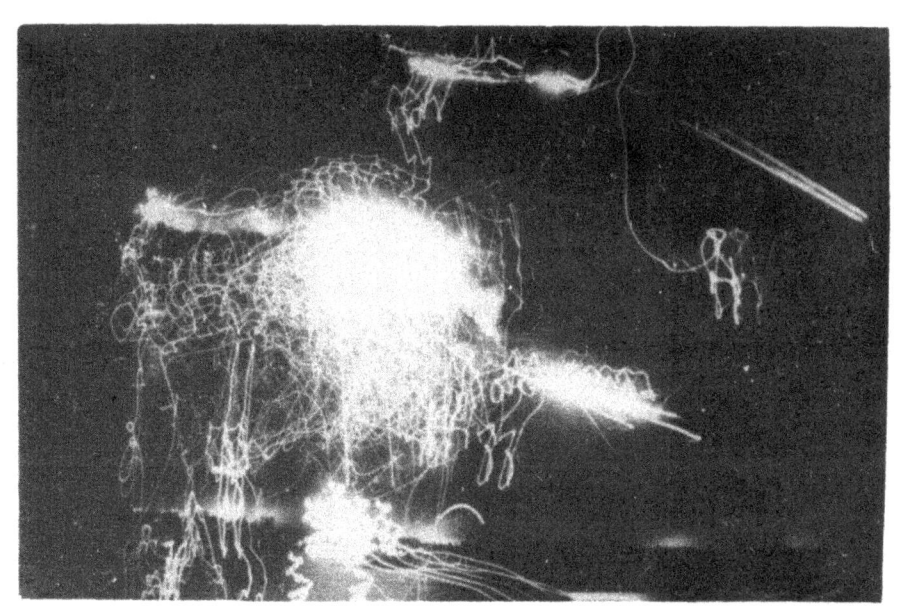

RETURN OF THE R.A.A.F. 1942

January, 1942, saw the return of the Australians and a visit by an American Boeing 314 *Clipper* flying boat, a contrast to the flight of the NC4. It was generally felt that a second R.A.A.F. Squadron was required so this was set in motion being formed out of the existing No. 10 and the newly-trained crews from the Empire Schools.

Possibly due to the concept that the Channel required cover, and mainly due to the overcrowding at Mount Batten, the new Squadron No. 461 was formed on 25th April and declared operational on 1st July. With the enemy forces now occupying the French bases along the Bay of Biscay, it seemed a strange choice of sites to locate the new Squadron at Poole but this is what happened on the 31st August.

No. 461 first saw action on the 8th July when their C.O. Wing Commander Halliday, R.A.F. set down and rescued the crew of a *Whitley* bomber. Squadron Leader Lovelock was the Flight Commander at this time. No. 10 had a share of action during these months and engaged two U boats, the U 71 and 105, and several blockade runners plus two Italian submarines. These were not without the loss of Flt.Lt. Judell on an Air Sea Rescue mission being shot down by an *Arado* 196 and July ended with another Sunderland failing to return from patrol. Before 461 departed they combined with No. 10 attacking a convoy.

August was another poor month for the Station. P.O. Buls of 461 on the 6th had rescued a crew but on the 10th Flt.Lt. Yeoman and his crew were lost and two days later W/Cdr. Halliday crashed whilst attempting to land for another downed crew. Sq.Ldr. Lovelock took over. September saw 461 still operating with the Sunderlands of No. 10. On the 1st two of 10s aircraft were joined by a 461 attack on Italian submarine and on the 9th a U boat was claimed and another severely damaged at the end of the month. 461 lost an aircraft at Hamworthy, their new base, on take off when it hit an obscured sand bank. Lacking any facilities Hamworthy was unpopular with all the Australians and they were thankful to move to Pembroke Dock some six months later but not before having to service the aircraft out in the open during the winter months without any hangarage or purpose-built building.

Mount Batten and the Plymothians took to the Australians and many links were forged which exist today. Like Pembroke Dock, the other main base, many friendships between the "dark blue boys" and the locals continued after the war and an exchange with local girls going to Australia and our Aussies settling over here resulted. It was during the next period of the war that the two Sunderland Squadrons were tested, although 461 had moved away. The close links between both continued and the Station played a major part in the events.

The Adversaries No. 1
SHORT SUNDERLAND MK III

British built flyingboat, R.A.F. Coastal Command, 1938-56, 749 aircraft were constructed. Served with Royal Air Force, Royal Australian Air Force, Royal Canadian Air Force, Royal Norwegian Air Force. Post-War: Royal Air Force, Royal New Zealand Air Force, French Navy, South African Air Force and three Squadrons operated in the Korean War.

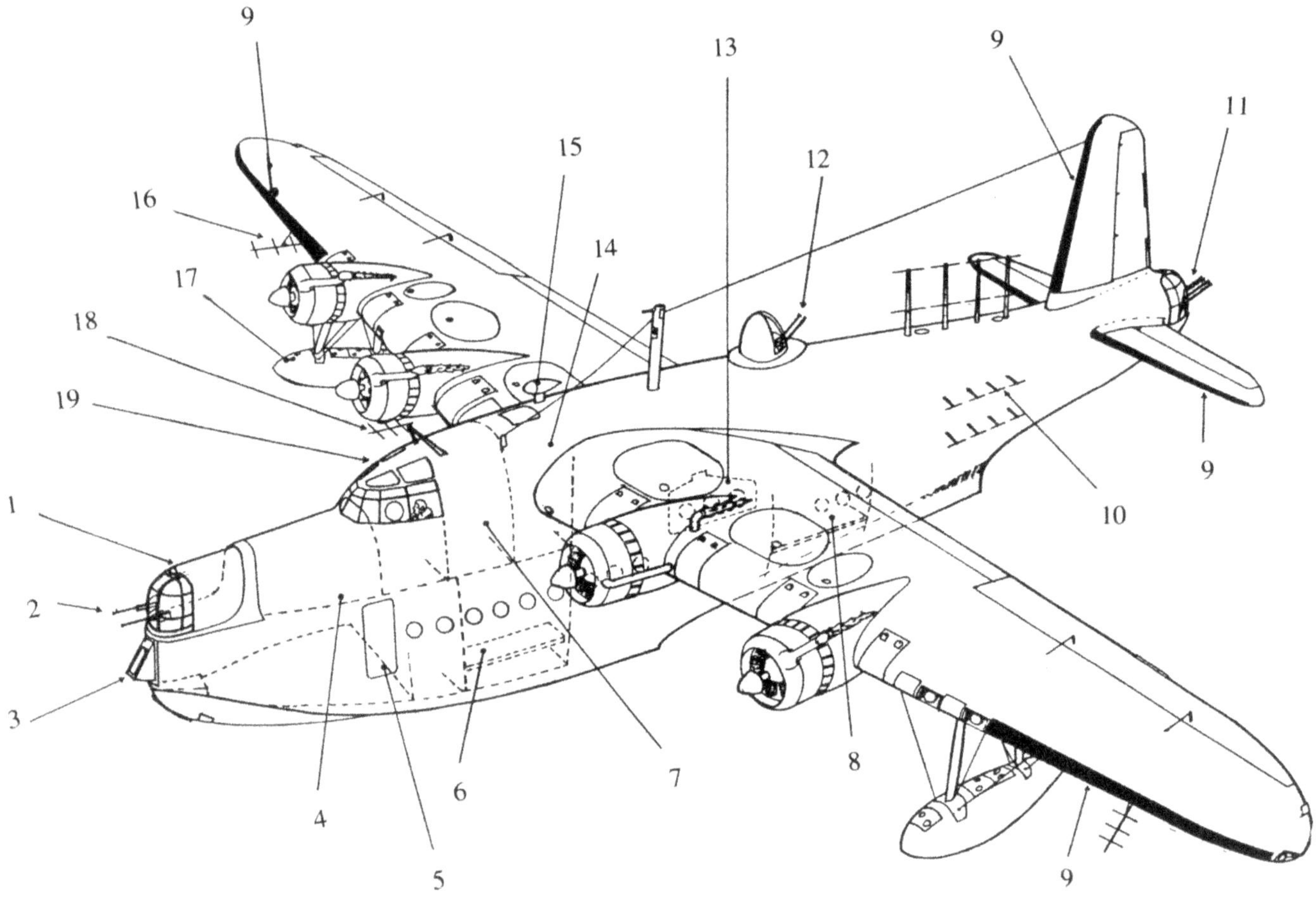

1. Retractable Front Turret
2. 2 x .303 mg
3. Bomb Aimer's Panel
4. Upper Floor
5. Door
6. Wardroom Bunks
7. Radio Operator
8. Crew Bunks
9. De-Icing Strips
10. A.S.V. Radar
11. 4 x .303 mg
12. 2 x .303 mg
13. Bomb Doors
14. Flight Engineer
15. D.F. Loop
16. Radar (YAGI)
17. Float
18. A.S.V. Radar
19. Cockpit

U243 under attack by W4030-H of 228 Squadron, R.A.F., and JM684-K of No. 10 Squadron on 8th July, 1944.

The Adversaries No. 2
GERMAN NAVAL U BOAT SUBMARINES

About 1,300 German submarines saw service and, combined with their Air Force, presented Britain with the most difficult foe which not only had to be destroyed but detected first. As the tactics of the Battle of the Atlantic changed so did the combatants' weapons and gradually reached maximums on both sides. Some 691 Mk.VIIc U boats were produced.

THE GERMAN U BOAT

Key to sketch drawings:
A. Type IX with 1 x 105mm forward, 1 x 37mm rear and two single 20mm guns
B. Type IX with 1 x 105mm, 1 x 37mm and a single 20mm
C. Type IX with 2 x 105mm and two single 20mm
D. Type IX with 2 x twin 20mm and a quadruple 20mm
E. Type IX with 2 x twin 20mm and a 37mm

Production of U boats was one of the main worries of the Allied Forces and whilst the Royal Navy and ships of the other nations took their toll of these submarines it was the aircraft which could provide long range detection and attack. In the early days it was sufficient to cause the U boat to dive and so interrupt the battery charging even if a direct attack was not possible. The German answer to this was to increase the anti-aircraft protection and fight it out on the surface.

Firepower

20mm gun, 450 rounds per minute, Range 2697/2950 yds
37mm gun, 160 rounds per minute, Range 6492m/2950 yds
20mm quadruple, 1800 rounds per minute, Range 2697m/2950 yds

The most numerous types were the Mk VIIc and the IXc

Data

Length	Range	Speed	Torpedos
VIIc 221 feet	8800 sea miles	18/7 knots	14 in 5 tubes
IXc 237 feet	13450 sea miles	18/7 knots	22 in 6 tubes

No. 10 Squadron in Action

U426 hit and sinking on 8th January, 1944. The *Sunderland*, EK586-U, which undertook this mission, was captained by F/O J.P. Roberts, F/O Ashdown, second pilot, F/O McPharlin, third pilot, F/O G.E. Rowe, navigator, Sgt. Portwine, Flt. Eng., F/Sgt. Dyer, Flt. Eng., F/Sgt. Randles, WOP/AG, Sgt. Robinson, second WOP/AG, F/Sgt. Spence, AG, F/Sgt. Goold, AG, Sgt. Morris, AG, made up the crew.

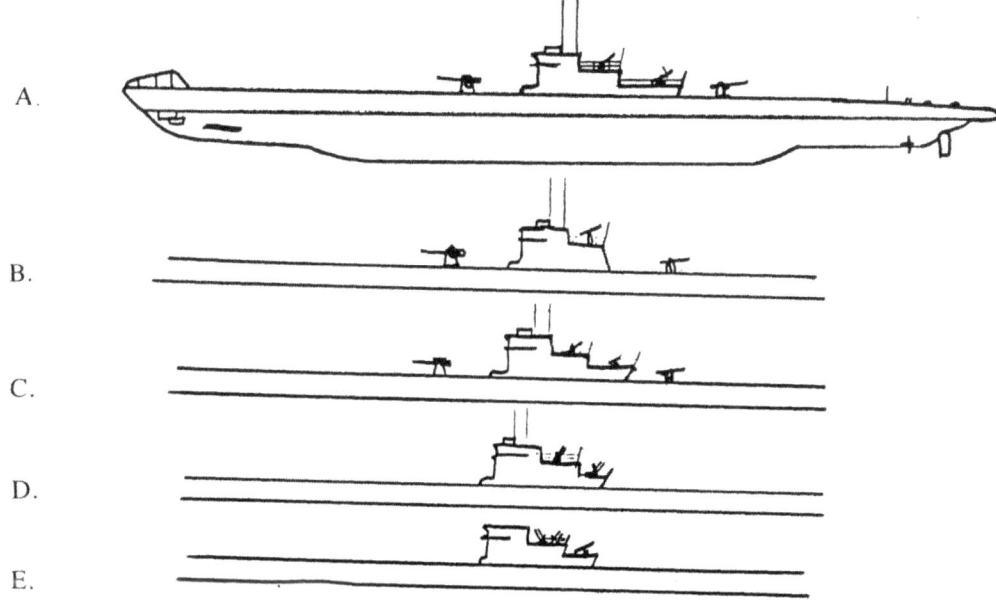

BATTLE OF THE ATLANTIC 1943

The height of the Battle of the Atlantic was being reached and at long last results were being achieved by both the land and sea-based aircraft of Coastal Command. It must be remembered that whilst this account is being written about the Station Mount Batten, the R.A.A.F. flying boat Squadrons were only a part of the Command's forces. Land-based aircraft at R.A.F. St. Eval, Davidstow Moor, Chivenor, Portreath, Predannack, Perranorth and the U.S. Navy at Dunkeswell contributed a major part with the Navy in destroying the U boat menace.

The Station's *Sunderlands* were to play an important role and achieve considerable success but not without loss. The diary of the year began with F/O Beeton sighting a blockade runner but not being able to sink it himself, he directed a naval vessel to the location to sink it. February saw a *Sunderland* fending off attacks by two FW 190s and then two Junkers 88s still managing to survive.

New tactics were being employed by the U boats in the same fashion that the Italians had adopted which was to stay on the surface and fight back. The Germans, however, mounted a battery of 20 mm cannon or mixtures of 20 and 30 mm behind the conning towers and this resulted in the loss of several flying boats.

May saw U563 sunk by a combined effort between No. 10 aircraft and another from 228 Squadron R.A.F. from Pembroke Dock. The numbers of submarines operating in the Atlantic had risen to about 130 and like the enemy fighters which now attacked in packs of four to six, so the U boats now hunted in packs of four or more. On the surface they could put up a solid barrage which kept aircraft at bay but it was the packs of Ju 88s which were causing the most concern, so much in fact that the R.A.F. employed packs of the splendid *Beaufighter* to minimise their effect. The Ju 88 has been many times described as the best all-round aircraft of World War Two and it was used as a bomber, dive bomber, fighter bomber, anti-shipping bomber, torpedo aircraft, day and night fighter and reconnaissance aircraft. It was armed with cannon and heavy machine guns which made it a very worthy opponent and in packs of up to nine the *Sunderlands* were faced with long odds but on most times acquitted themselves well, even those which were shot down took two or three of the enemy with them.

July saw a *Sunderland* fighting off four attackers and it is likely that these Ju 88s were in the pack that attacked another of our machines which encountered seven Ju 88s and returned home on the 3rd August., A gallant attack was made on 1st August by Flt.Lt. Fry flying RB-B (W4020) when he sighted U454 commanded by Kapitan Hacklander.

From a distance of about a mile and a half Fry commenced a long low attack and was punished by accurate cannon fire from the 1 x 37 mm cannon at long range plus four 20 mm cannon as the range closed. The fuel tanks were punctured and the cockpit repeatedly hit but Fry dropped his depth charges from only 50 feet and U454 was destroyed. RB-B continued for a while until crashing into the sea and breaking up, six of the crew were rescued but not the gallant Fry.[1]

August had seen twenty-five U boats sunk by Coastal Command aircraft three of which the No. 10 Squadron's aircraft had accounted for but eight of the aircraft were lost resulting in four machine guns being installed in the nose of *Sunderlands* to clear the decks of enemy gunners and it worked.

Once a very well known sight to the citizens of Plymouth, aircraft at their moorings on the Cattewater.

NORMANDY LANDINGS 1944

This year was to see the height reached prior to the Allied landings of "D" Day, 6th June, and two responsibilities were placed upon Coastal Command. One was to free the Atlantic of supply-carrying ships for the invasion and secondly to clear the Channel of U boats to prevent any attacks upon the troopships and store carriers. Mount Batten became a focal point for both operations. However, the Australians were mainly concerned in the operations against the Japanese in the Pacific and so on the 27th January six *Sunderlands* were sent to Australia just about five years late on delivery! Four more followed in February and a lot of the veterans returned after giving excellent service over here. Machines and crews were more plentiful but the limits were stretched in hunting the U boats and preventing them from getting from the Atlantic to the Channel.

On the 8th January F/O Roberts sank the U426 and a combined attack by F/O Tilley with a 228 Squadron's aircraft sank the U243 but these were exceptions. Plymouth Sound filled up with invasion craft and landings or take-offs were very difficult and at one time aircraft were diverted. As "D" Day approached 92 operational flights were recorded totalling 1,146 flying hours without a sighting in June. July saw 945 hours flown for one success, the U243, but the object of the exercise was achieved and the troopships were free of U boat attacks.

The enemy went north and so did the hunters but fifty-eight patrols in August followed by fifty-one in September and forty-eight in December tells its own story.

Accidents seemed to have taken over from No. 10's action and during the year eight *Sunderlands* were lost, including ML839 which was one of two standard aircraft machines which were re-engined by the Australians with American Pratt and Whitney engines which sank in a gale but was recovered. This re-engining was to result in the makers producing aircraft with American engines as Mk Vs.

Groundcrews: Whilst it is natural to report on the work of the aircrews' exploits and no one would wish to detract from their achievements and few would want to change places with them risking almsot certain death either in the air or sea, those ground crews who toiled in freezing conditions or struggled out on the wings when it was blowing and raining must be remembered in the same context. The aircrews themselves have mentioned over and over to me not to omit the team of men and women who kept them up there. Everyone played their parts and must not be forgotten.

The gathering of ships in Plymouth Sound for "D" Day, 6th June, 1944, presented great difficulties to the flying boats landing and taking off and the barrage balloons didn't help at all.

Sunderlands Overhead

The endless patrolling either of submarine hunting or convoy escorting; worthwhile noting are the two old Royal Navy destroyers probably, H or I class, with another vessel in the foreground.

Barrage Balloon Unit No. 934 or 964 at Mount Batten

Servicing Planes

In the early days the crews themselves were trained so that they could undertake most of the day to day servicing of the aircraft and it was only when required that the aircraft were beached and major repairs carried out. As the pace of the war quickened, ground crews took over these tasks and worked 11 hour days, seven days a week which increased to 15 hour days in the busy periods on a basic wage with no overtime. Although these pictures were of the members of No. 10 Squadron, Royal Australian Air Force, quite a large number of R.A.F. tradesmen served with both Australian Squadrons. Working at that height from the ground or over the sea any tools which were dropped or accidents usually had serious results (top photo Western Morning News).

An Australian with the dark blue forage cap busy on a *Sunderland* engine early in the war. Note the well worn gills and scuff marks.

MARINE CRAFT AND CREWS

The following six photographs from Mr. A.R.J. Cowell illustrate the various types of marine craft used by the Royal Air Force units at flying boat bases.

Then Flt.Sgt. Cowell, A.R.J. on Pinnace No. 17, seen here leaving the marine dock in 1941. Good detail of the hatchway and its high surround can be seen, the universal greatcoat and forage cap were standard wear.

A most interesting shot of the dock and occupants. The bottom left corner is home to a Bomb Scow used for rearming the aircraft. Left of centre is part of Pinnace No. 17 and in front of this the refuelling vessel can be made out with two planing dinghies tied up to it. These smaller craft were used for ferrying the crews to the flying boats. Top right Pinnace No. 15 is moored up in front of the Seaplane tender.

Pinnace Crew in 1941

The crew photographed on Pinnace No. 15. As can be seen "clothes various" was the dress of the day. The date is 1941. Pinnaces were the backbone of the A.S.R. Units around the south-west in the early days of the war and served on most Stations or detachments. Mr. Cowell notes that the two 56 foot Pinnaces, Nos. 15 and 17, were on Station with No. 204 Squadron's *Saro Londons* during 1938 and continued on serving.

Ferry Boats from Plymouth

Three Ferryboats with romantic names, *Rapid*, *Swift* and *Lively*, were the main link from R.A.F. Mount Batten and Plymouth and were much in demand. As can be seen, there was always a rush to get on and off. The ferry service continued long after the war had ended but gradually, the numbers of passengers dropped due to bus services and the ferry boats were finally scrapped.

The Marine Dock

Another shot of the marine dock with a wealth of information and detail. In the bottom left corner the seaplane tender is behind Refueller, No. 1197, on the left with another seaplane tender alongside it. The larger Pinnace, No. 15, occupies the top right hand corner with another Bomb Scow in the bottom right of the photograph whilst several planing dinghies are to be seen in the centre.

Air Sea Rescue Unit No. 43

Two of the vessels of the Air Sea Rescue Unit, No. 43, alongside the breakwater in 1944. The high speed launch was capable of a considerable turn of speed and were good sea boats if uncomfortable at low engine revolutions. Like all designs of this type, once the planing speed has been reached the vessel would give a maximum performance. Note the revolving circular windscreen wipes which could cope with most conditions of spray by spinning the water off.

ACCIDENTS

No matter how well organised any unit is there is almost always a joker in the pack called *accident*. In the case of aviation weather is acceptable, mechanical failure something to be taken in the stride but losses due to events which are *beyond expectation will take place and usually are put down* to accident in the official records which normally only covers the bare outlines. In Scotland one of No. 10's aircraft was lost landing at night when the line of flare boats drifted inshore and the aircraft ploughed onto the rocks.

Sudden gales claimed numerous aircraft and in many cases fate took a hand by driving ships which had broken free of their moorings across those of the aircraft and ripped them apart, the result being the aircraft landing up as wrecks on the rocks. Fire is another hazard which can start with no one in sight and incinerate an aircraft in minutes; ironically it was accidents which claimed as many *Sunderlands* in the last year of operations as had been lost in action.

The following photographs have come from many amateur sources and today record the losses which otherwise are just entries in a book. Possibly the most hair-raising accident recorded was when the inner propellor sheared off, missing *the pilot and cart-wheeled across the top of the wings* damaging the flaps and finally disappeared over the side just in front of the tail plane. Some crashes had ironic twists. An aircraft, force-landed on take off and crash-landed; it began to sink so a rescue boat went out and as it picked up survivors the depth charges in the aircraft set to explode at a certain depth went up and killed everyone. A very high tide claimed another aircraft when a visiting aircraft landed the seaward side of the Breakwater on what appeared to be a long stretch of sea but, in fact, the water was up to the level of the stonework and only inches deep, the aircraft foundered on the rocks.

29th March, 1943. *Sunderland* 'V' of No. 119 Squadron R.A.F. had to divert to the Station and force-landed in the Cattewater itself. These amateur photographs record the aircraft in the centre with spray issuing forth. The marine craft went to the rescue and stood by the aircraft which took on a lot of water and was in danger of sinking.

The crew and others had to go out and sit on the opposite wing to prevent the aircraft turning over and sinking and can be seen doing this. Note the float has been ripped off and she finally settled level and was brought ashore.

V-119 Squadron. Devoid of as much as can be removed the flying boat settled and can be seen on a fairly level keel.

ML 839 a *Sunderland* Mk.III being raised after a severe drenching. A victim of a strong gale combined with a doorway not being securely fastened, this famous aircraft sank overnight. This was the aircraft which had American engines fitted locally and the modification was adopted by the makers. Date 12th October, 1944.

ML 829 coming up. The aircraft was making a normal take off when she failed to rise and stalled into the sea but it had to be on top of the anti-submarine defences and she hit the boom and sank. Date 9th February, 1945. Note the Breakwater behind the anti-submarine nets.

Aircraft DD852 was at her moorings when a ship passed too close and cut the ropes causing the aircraft to be blown on to the rocks. Date 2nd April, 1944. In these cases not often were the aircraft recoverable so the ground crews had to work at high speed to recover all the valuable equipment.

All flying boats tend to sit on the surface of the sea and have very little draught, the 25-30 tons being spread over quite a lot of area. This coupled with their slab-sided construction made them very prone to being blown adrift during gales. This picture shows a machine wrecked on the shore, the fuselage has almost gone and only the main spar with some frames remains.

Fire is always a hazard and it doesn't take long for it to get a good hold. A Mk.III JM678 was being serviced when fire broke out probably due to a short in the electrics and it quickly spread to the combustible and fuel areas. In a short while there was very little left of the plane. Date 19th June, 1944.

END OF HOSTILITIES 1945

Even though the end of the war was in sight, the patrolling had to be undertaken as the U boats had returned to the south-western area again. For a few months it was the task of locating them and then when the peace came of rounding them up as they surrendered. Accidents claimed two more of No. 10's aircraft. ML 829 was taking off in Plymouth Sound in a cross wind when she bounced and despite the pilot's efforts failed to climb and fell back striking the anti-submarine net. She broke in half killing two of the crew with six more injured.

No. 10 Squadron departed from Plymouth for Australia in October, 1945, having flown 4,553,860 miles on 3,177 operations and had sunk 5 U boats. It was with mixed feelings that the "Aussies" departed, glad to be going home but with the war against the Japanese an unpleasant prospect still facing them. Plymouth had taken to these cheery crowd from "Down Under" and this has been reflected with the return visits that the Sunderlanders' Association have been making every few years to visit the old base.

The only evidence in Plymouth that the Australians were based in the City during the war, a plaque on the Barbican overlooking the Mayflower Stone.

Cleaning up before going home. The R.A.A.F. cleared up the Station with the aid of a tractor and a lot of humour!

Victory march past March, 1945. Civic dignitaries joined Service Officers acknowledging the part that the R.A.A.F. and Mount Batten had played in the vital defence of our shipping lanes during the war.

THE AUSSIES

One of the only good things to come out of war are the fellowships which are formed and even after very many years incidents are recalled. Here we have the usual one for the family album. "Thats me Mum, with me mates." Usually heavily scribed on the back with names such as *Bodger, Monkey,* and *Roo* we are none the wiser now!

Another of the ground crew photographs this time without any clues as to the identity of the trio. However, without them and the many others there is no way that the flying boats could have operated. Accounts of the aircrews achievements can be found but very little is recorded about the ground crew's work in all kinds of weather often out on wings over the sea where a false step could end in an icy ducking or wade into chest-high sea to fix the beaching gear to the *Sunderlands.* The average day for these crews was from 0800 hours to 2300 which, in the quiet periods, was reduced from 15 hours to only 11 per day, seven days a week, naturally.

No. 10 Squadron on parade in front of the large hangars with two *Sunderlands* in the background.

No. 10 group photograph in front of a *Sunderland*. No details are known but one assumes this was taken in 1943 from the paint finish on the aircraft.

Celebration party, one of the more pleasant ways of spending a war.

Members of No. 10 Squadron Mount Batten

Left to right: Flt. Lt. Strath, Flt. Lt. Rossiter, F/O Woodland, Sqn. Ldr. Egerton, D.F.C., F/O Wilson, Wg. Cdr. Rice, A.V.M. Wrigley, C.B.E., D.F.C., A.F.C., A.V.M. Durston, C.B., A.F.C., R.A.F., Flt. Lt. Farmer, A.V.M. Baker, C.B., D.S.O., M.C., A.F.C., R.A.F., Sqn. Ldr. Patherick. Note the shoulder flashes "Australia" and the small metal eagle badges over cuff stripes on R.A.A.F.

POST-WAR

After the Australians had departed the Station was taken over by No. 238 Maintenance Unit who remained until September, 1953. Their job of keeping the Station on a reserve footing and as a store, meant that the *Sunderlands* of the R.A.F. based at Calshot and Pembroke Dock could still return right up to 1958. No. 238 were replaced by the Marine Craft Training School using many of the vessels which had seen wartime use. This Unit came down from Calshot and were to be on Station for over thirty years.

In 1961 it was decided to make the base the principal Station of the R.A.F. Marine Branch and the old hangars and slipways were to have their new areas for maintenance and training of the vessels and crews of the Marine Squadrons. These were employed on target towing and Air Sea Rescue although this role was being taken over by the helicopters. Training of boats crews for postings home and abroad were undertaken and the boats also took part in exercises with the School of Survival, another of the Station's residents. Three sections of the Marine Branch existed working with each other. The Engineering Branch, as it's name implies, undertook the servicing of the vessels and transport whilst the other Squadrons, the Administration and Supply, were self explanatory.

The School of Survival

All aircrews have to undergo each year a course of survival training and at Mount Batten there were the facilities for both the elements of ditching at sea, airlifting by helicopter and the privations of being left out on nearby Dartmoor. Working with the helicopters from R.A.F. Chivenor, No. 22 Squadron's 'A' Flight, they were placed in the sea to undertake dinghy and liferaft drill before the standby chopper took them to dry off. Life on the moors was considerably rougher having to construct one's own shelter and survive all the unpleasantness. The course covered worldwise types of survival and paid off good results as did the wartime ones. Today the Marine branch has been run down and the School of Survival moved away.

A good photograph of HMAFV 2513 with Plymouth Hoe in the background. These fast launches were the backbone of the Air Sea Rescue service; fine sea boats, they had a good turn of speed.

"Up he comes." The two crew members in the liferaft are demonstrating how to bring another aboard by pulling up on the harness of the life jacket or "Mae West", not an easy job when there is a sea running and it is cold. Righting a large life raft by oneself is a difficult job at any time. The idea is to swim under and out to find a rope then clamber up and by hauling on the rope lift the nose as one leans back. Unfortunately the suction created by the upper covering being immersed in the sea, usually requires several attempts and feels like it is anchored taking considerable effort to right.

HELICOPTER AIR SEA RESCUE

The first signs of rescue craft came at the end of the First World War when harbour launches were kept in reserve for this purpose and during the years between the wars high-speed launches were developed and kept on station as the cost of machines and men became excessive. Men were no longer expendible and a trained man was hard to replace so gradually high speed launches were produced. Like many things it was the war which gave a sense of urgency to Air Sea Rescue which combined both special air search and sea rescue. Pilots which could be saved lived to fight again and Mount Batten came into it's own controlling craft around the shores plus aircraft kept at Harrowbeer and the station's own aircraft.

The end of the war saw the marine craft settling down to a quiet time but a new form of rescue was to take over in the shape of the helicopter. Developed during the latter stages, it came into it's own in the Korean War and for the first time units were formed to rescue downed pilots behind enemy lines and in the oceans. By the mid-1950s the R.A.F. too had their own helicopters and No. 22 Squadron had flights around the coasts. "A" Flight at Chivenor, in North Devon, had *Whirlwind* helicopters and had the distinction of flying the last of this type on search and rescue duties. These were the HAR 10s.

In the photographs are XP346 seen outside the Officers Mess and one on exercise with the School of Survival. In this picture you can see the winchman being lowered carrying a stretcher whilst the navigator in the doorway directs the pilot. The winchman wears an immersible suit. The last of these exercises took place on the 28th January, 1986, when HMAFV *Halifax* 4003 deposited aircrew into the sea and waited for the helicopter to airlift them back onboard. As fate would have it the very reliable *Wessex* developed trouble and landed at Mount Batten so the last exercise was completed by boat.

A fine photograph of Wessex XV720 from "A" Flight, No. 22 Squadron, Chivenor, carrying out the last A.S.R. exercise with HMAFV 4003 manned by an R.A.F. Marine craft section crew. This took place in January, 1986, in Plymouth Sound beyond which can be seen the headland of Rame Head in Cornwall.

Commissioning Ceremony

The commission of HMA.F.V. *Seagull*, No. 5001, and a shot of Seal 5000 at sea illustrates the lines of these boats. The hull is black with pale blue grey upperworks.

STATION BUILDINGS AND THEIR USE

Looking at the photographs in this section it is not hard to realise that basically the area consists of a huge stony outcrop with the tower built on it and the surrounding low land rising gently up to the high ground on the cliff tops at the southern limits of the area. The normal prevailing wind is from the south-west which determined all the hangars to be built with the door openings facing away from this direction. The original buildings for R.A.F. Mount Batten were erected prior to the Second World War and therefore the Officers' Mess and other buildings conform with the very recognisable architectural fashion of those days with red brick work being the style. After all these years this has mellowed considerably and now blends in very well with the surrounding large grass areas.

The main hangars were re-cladded a few years ago along with the other workshops and buildings in the northern corner including the rather rare north-light construction which, whilst found in numerous factories outside the Services, is not often applied to airfield buildings except the few hangars with roofs like this with brick built walls. Of special interest in this corner is the old white and red brick building dating back to the days of 1915-16. We know that a fish canning factory was built around this site and that the R.N.A.S. was built alongside it taking it over when the business closed and the area became a Royal Naval establishment but nothing has been produced to establish whether or not this is the building which was the factory which became the first Naval permanent structure. There is no doubt that wooden huts were erected around this site at the same time. It certainly resembles other factories built at that time. Alongside there are the engine test sheds and on the side opposite the north light buildings, is the gymnasium.

From the tower looking down one can see in an anti-clock direction the No. 2 hangar which served almost all its life as a Motor Transport repair and servicing shed which it shared during the war with marine craft. Alongside that today are stores which were built after the hangar was bombed and destroyed. This No. 1 hangar standing on the site of a timber construction housed the *Short* 184s operating during the First World War. Tracks on the stone jetty carried a steam crane. The traces can still be seen where these were. The first permanent hangars are thought to have been built during the early 1930s or late 1920s probably spread over a few years whilst the rest of the Station's buildings were being constructed, such as the quarters for single officers. Hut accommodation was later replaced by the brick structures and the workshops. Leaving No. 1 site, there are the yellow painted meteorological buildings which housed these very important people for many years until they moved to their present position at the top of the hill.

Barrack blocks occupy the area south of the tower whilst on the same level as the base of the tower there are the remains of the Station identification letter-square which used to house ZB, the code letters. Nearer the tower is a static water tank and the flag pole on which the R.A.F. Ensign flies. Looking south-west one can see the famous Drake's Island, well known to many visitors to Plymouth Hoe, and due south is the Breakwater which was the southern limit of the *Sunderlands* landing and take off strips. In the area between the sea and the Officers' Mess are the cliffs with beaches at the bottom and the long rock outcrops on which quite a few aircraft foundered over the years. Looking south-east over the main hangars one can see the mess surrounded by well-kept grass with the slopes rising up behind. Facing south-west the mess came in for a fair share of gales and winter weather and the long distance to the aircraft didn't make it over popular but the past occupants regard it with affection.

Out of sight from the tower to the south-east there is the guard house through which all pass, except by air. There are still a few which come this way in the helicopter from R.A.F. Chivenor for their survival courses or on communication flights. Still in the south-east sector is the marine dock completed in 1933 and due east are the two main hangars which strangely are considered by many of the later entrants of the R.A.F. to have nothing to do with anything except marine craft! The large sheds used to accommodate *Sunderlands* and *Catalinas* which were towed up the long slipways now used by the Marine Section who lift the vessels out of the sea at the Point.

There are, of course, many other buildings sheltering in the lea of the rock such as the huts of the School of Survival and the NCO Mess. Today, with the proposed closure, it is hard to realise that all the years of R.A.F. occupation is coming to an end. The view to the east and north-east is of a fine stretch of water (Cattewater) sheltered both by the breakwater or stone pier and the rock. A yachting marina is being developed here. Whatever happens it will always be remembered. It has a place in history. The demise of the flying boat was the beginning of the end for the Station. It's occupants were later the marine craft, these disbanded as a Section on 8th Janury, 1986.

A strange twist of fate will continue the saga of the Pembroke Dock stained-glass window. At the end of World War Two the fine window was dedicated in the small church on the base at Pembroke Dock in Wales and depicted the Squadrons which operated from there such as 461 R.A.A.F. and the Canadians. However, the R.A.F. closed the base and the window was removed to safety at Mount Batten, it being installed in the Officers' Mess. In 1983 a move was made by the council of Pembroke Dock to regain the window but this was resisted and as time went on it looked as if the window would stay on R.A.F. soil. The announced closure now makes it certain that the window will return to Wales. Looking back over the years Mount Batten has served the country well in two World Wars and maintained a high standard in the peace.

Bird Class Sea-Going Vessels

Sea Otter, one of the class of sea-going vessels built for the Royal Navy and Royal Air Force. The naval ones, being named Bird Class, *Kingfisher*, *Cygnet*, *Petrel*, *Sandpiper* and *Sea Otter*, seen here awaiting disposal, has now become H.M.S. *Redpole* having joined the others in this fishery protection class, a change from the long range recovery purpose. The lower picture shows the beaching cradles used to bring up the vessels for repairs on shore.

The Station Headquarters with the Meteorological offices

The heart of any Station is the H.Q. Block within which the administration and day to day running of the base is carried out. R.A.F. Mount Batten has been the home of the Meteorological office for very many years and another photograph in this book shows the original buildings at the end of the stone jetty. Together with R.A.F. St. Mawgan, much data is collected and passed on to the various interested bodies; it contributes to the much maligned weather forecast as broadcast by the T.V. networks, the newspapers and individual requirements.

Guard House

The first place anyone entering the Station arrives at. Here one has to state their business and obtain permission to enter. This one, of a fairly old pattern, is typical of many and has a road barrier; note the fire alarm bell.

Old R.N.A.S. Buildings

Royal Naval Air Service buildings. The top picture shows an interesting building which could possibly be the oldest on the Station as all evidence points to this as being the fish-processing plant which existed in 1913. It is known to have been used later as a workshop, a role which has remained up to 1986. Of interest is the lintel over the bricked-up doorways which appears to have been an afterthought. It's appearance is very much that of an old engine shed as used by the railways. It is most certainly the best of the R.N.A.S. Cattewater buildings. In the lower picture the other engine testing building can be seen against the background of the Cattewater and Sutton harbour.

Round Tower and Stores Buildings

The old limestone tower dominates the area and here can be seen looming over the stores in the upper picture. These Second World War structures and some original 1928 buildings, have all been recladded to extend their lives. In the lower picture the wartime gymnasium is the building on the left this, today, is now used for storage.

Officers' Mess

Typical of many structures erected in the mid-1930s, the messes conform to a standard pattern. Although the surroundings may alter the layout of rooms, with sleeping accommodation in the end blocks, the general layout made it possible to almost always find one's way around. In the rear of the view shown, a sea view was enjoyed for so many years by residents which was considered to be unequalled in any R.A.F. station. The lower photograph shows one of the older wooden buildings to be found still in use and is typical of early guard-houses. In the rear can be seen one of the brick-built barrack blocks also dating from the 1930s.

General Views over the Station

The main hangars in which the flying boats were serviced in latter years were later the home of the marine craft for major servicing and were recladded and modernised. Alongside these can be seen the older training blocks and, in the left corner, the N.C.O.'s mess. Turnchapel with small boat moorings can also be seen in the background. The lower picture shows the last of the twelve radio masts which were for so long a most distinctive land mark standing on ground at Staddon Heights.

Marine Craft and Marine Dock

No. 1390 craft is on a trolley in front of the main hangars; the hull colours are black with brick-red underneath, the cheat-line being white. Upper colours are pale blue grey with white roof. The numbers also are in white. These boats are the oldest in the R.A.F. service.

The date on the wall below says 1933 and tells us when the Marine Dock was constructed but not a lot has changed. Gone are the steam-craft but the small boats, like No. 2002 seen in the photograph, existed up to mid-1986. The wooden building reminds one of an office for boat trips!

Then and now

Although over forty years separate these pictures it is interesting to compare what is still remaining. The stone jetty over the last few years became disused for the first time in it's long existance. During the 1939-45 war it was the home of the barrage balloons with several occupants such as "W" Flight of No. 934 Squadron as shown here.

Plymouth Hoe in 1940 shows the famous lighthouse and, in front of that, the pier which was destroyed during the blitz and a *Sunderland*. Air Sea Rescue craft and marine craft are in the other photograph showing the Hoe as seen from Mount Batten tower with the famous Barbican from whence the Mayflower sailed and Sir Francis Drake returned from his voyages around the world.

Winter and Summer at the Station

Complete contrasts are shown here. In the top wartime picture several interesting features can be seen. The stone pier which can be seen to the top right of the picture has changed little from today as can be noted in the photograph on the next page. However, the hangar alongside it was destroyed in 1940. The windsock located top right moved post-war to near the Officers' Mess for the helicopters. In the centre of the photograph can be seen the station's identification square the remains of which can be seen in the lower photograph which incidentally was taken during 1984's severe drought. Nothing remains of the small buildings in the upper left corner. The lower picture shows the re-located mast with the R.A.F. ensign flying and a "S" Class British submarine passing Mount Batten in safety.

Views from the Wartime years and 1984

Cold comfort — a *Catalina* in front of a *Sunderland* in the background of this rather wintery shot. The men are standing in front of the *Castle* pub. Note the main hangars and, just visible on top of the snow-covered hill, are the twelve radio masts. Winter not only reduced the flying hours but also hindered the servicing. The modern photograph shows the re-cladded hangars with the renewed concrete front apron which has slipways down to the water. Usually three flying boats were kept in each hangar as a maximum but as the needs were so great it was normal to have as few as possible and, therefore, only one or two machines would be having major overhauls at the same time.

The Foreshore in the Wartime and Pier in 1984

In the top photograph one can see little difference in comparison with today except for minor alterations. One deletion is the anti-aircraft gun position in front of the Officers' Mess on the cliff top. In the lower view one can see the buildings against the quay wall replacing the destroyed No. 1 hangar and No. 2 in the right hand corner. As time went on post-war buldings were modified for new use and the Station's transport section occupied No. 2 up to the end of its service life.

Views in 1945 and 1984

Apart from a lot of tree growth the scene is much the same. Sadly we no longer have *Sunderlands* flying. This one is RB-A of No. 10 R.A.A.F. and the date is 1945, but at least we have two in museums. One could be forgiven for thinking that the cannon in the bottom left hand corner of the 1985 photograph is what we are reduced to for defence now but these are in the top of the 1660s tower and keep a look out for us. It is now that one wonders what the fate of this area will be in another forty years.

A French built Atlantic serving NATO with the German Navy under the command of SOUMAR.

THE POST-WAR YEARS

These saw the station reverting back to a training role and although, without the aircraft, it kept an operational force of marine craft combining training and standby, plus the vital crew-training work in Air Sea Rescue as part of the survival exercises.

It also has been the home of the Royal Air Force Auxillary Unit which keen persons, both ex-service and civilian, work together undertaking tasks which their counterparts carry out in the R.A.F. These "week-enders", as they became known, came into being after the war had ended and several Squadrons of *Vampire* and *Meteor* fighters were formed under the Auxillary title with ground crews and other supporting activities. However, defence cuts in the 1950s brought about the demise of these units.

Many considered that this was a bad move remembering, that at the beginning of the War in 1939, the Volunteer and Auxilliaries were depended upon to man the fighters. The excuse was the cost of crew-training and flying. Today it is considered that many tasks should be covered by well-trained part-timers who, in the event of an emergency, could take over as they do when they go to annual camp.

The Meteorological office used to be sited close to the pier but later moved to higher ground. It has been suggested that this was so that they didn't suffer from the bad weather they didn't forecast! Anyhow for very many years they have provided the information which appears on television and sound broadcasts plus being part of the national set up, information is recorded and kept in an effort to maintain the standard that they have become known for. This data has provided much valuable information to very many occupations such as farming and sporting activities, etc.

Mount Batten will have existed in one form or another for seventy-three years and no matter what may be in store for this site it has a place in the history of Britain which cannot be replaced or equalled.

SOUMAR: The Southern Maritime Air Region

Another of the Station's functions was as the Headquarters of the Commander Maritime Air Sub Area and also the Headquarters, combining with the Royal Navy, Operational.

The Southern Maritime Air and the Navy covered all maritime air-sea activities south of a line approximately 54°N from the North Sea to the Atlantic and came, in turn, under No. 18 Group based in London. SOUMAR was formed in 1941 as 19 Group Area Combined Headquarters on the 5th February, 1941, taking up residence in an old fort on the boundary of the city. The chain of forts were constructed for an earlier defence system, however, and they served SOUMAR well during the very heavy blitz raids of 1941 and afterwards. The operations block at Eggbuckland Keep survived as did the administration offices at Mount Wise. The following year 1942, saw the construction underground of a new complex which housed all the units which has been there ever since as the Area Combined Headquarters.

No. 19 Group during the War played a major part in the Battle of the Atlantic and the aircraft, both land and sea-based, took a large toll of enemy submarines and blockade runners. In 1943 members of the United States Naval Office took up residence with special interest concerning the Fleet Air Wing which operated aircraft from Dunkeswell.

The War over, No. 19 Groups aircraft comprised of *Lancaster* ASR 3/MR3s at St. Eval near Newquay, *Sunderlands* at Mount Batten and Pembroke Dock and communication aircraft (*Anson* and *Austers*) at Roborough, Plymouth. Apart from the exercises with the Royal Navy and Air Sea Rescue the main task was the meteorological flights for the Met. Office at Mount Batten and St. Eval. *Sunderlands* did operate on airlift of supplies to Berlin when the Russians blockaded the city in 1948. In April, 1949, NATO was formed and No. 19 took on the responsibilities of Air Command Central Atlantic and Sub-Area of the Channel.

The Korean War which commenced in 1950, saw Coastal Command regain some of its wartime importance and St. Mawgan re-opened again as the Maritime Training School and the School of Anti-Submarine/Sea Warfare Development Unit with *Lancaster* and, later, *Shackletons*. The last of the *Sunderland* units were disbanded in 1957 at Pembroke Dock but a few French and other machines did visit up to early 1958.

During the mid-1950s helicopters began to replace the fixed-wing aircraft in the A.S.R. role. *Sycamores* were the first of these in Coastal Command service at St. Mawgan but later in 1959 *Whirlwinds* had replaced the 275 Squadron's aircraft and one of the best known and long lasting associations began when No. 22 Squadron 'A' Flight based at R.A.F. Chivenor, flew their all yellow *Whirlwinds*. They are still there today and likely to be for many more years having only a few years ago exchanged their HAR 10s for *Wessex*. They even remained when their Station closed down and their bond with the residents of the North Coasts of Cornwall and Devon is very strong. 1969 saw Coastal Command disbanded and absorbed into SOUMAR of 18 Group taking in NATO. This organisation lasted until 1984 when it was disbanded. The Royal Air Force Auxiliaries are still at the Base but with an uncertain future, it is difficult to predict what will happen.

APPENDIX

NOTE. The British Standards Institute denote the differences between seaplanes as: *Floatplanes and Flying Boats or Float seaplanes and Boat seaplanes* this being the terms applied to aircraft which can take off from water either by floats or having a boat shaped fuselage. In the following list floatplanes are denoted with an asterisk*. All the other aircraft are flying boats.

Aircraft types known to have been at the Station.
RNAS Cattewater
*Short 184, N1099, N1142, N1624, N1796, N2836, N2959, N1601. *Hamble Baby, *Sopwith Baby, Large America.

R.A.F. Cattewater
*Short 184/23 Sq., *Short 240/237 Sq., Felixstowe F2A/238 Sq., Felixstowe F3/238 Sq., Felixstowe F5/238 Sq.

R.A.F. Mount Batten
Southampton I/203 Sq., S1301.
Southampton II/203.S1232.
Scapa/204.
Perth/209.
Southampton Mk X/203 Sq.
*Fairey IIID/204 Sq.
Blackburn Iris/209 Sq. S1263.
*Fairey IIIF/444 Flt.R.N. J9794.
Saro London/204 K6927, K5911, K6930, K5913, K6930.
*Hawker Osprey/407 Flt.R.N.
*Wapiti J9498.
Stranraer 209 Sq./K7280.
*Swordfish K8429.
*Shark/No. 2 Anti-aircraft co operation unit.
Sunderland/204 Sq.R.A.F. L2158, L5799, L5802, N9021, N9024, N9028, N9030, N9044, N9046, T9070, T9072.
Sunderland/228 R.A.F. N9029, P9600, W3989, W4032.
Sunderland/442 R.Canadian A.F. ML884, EJ151.
Sunderland/461 R.Australian A.F. L5802, T9090, T9109, T9111, T9113, T9114, T9115.
Sunderland/No.10 Sq.R.A.A.F. N9048, N9049, N9050, P9600, P9601, P9602, P9603, P9604, P9605, P9606, T9047, T9071, T9072, T9075, T9086, T9110, W3979, W3983, W3984, W3985, W3986, W3993, W3994, W3997, W3999, W4003, W4004, W4019, W4020, W4024, W4030, W6054, DD852, DD865, DD867, DP177, DP179, DB192, DV958, DV959, DV993, DW113, EK572, EK574, EK575, EK586, EK594, JM678, JM684, JM685, JM686, JM721, ML813, ML822, ML828, ML829, ML830, ML831, ML839, ML848, ML856, NJ193, NJ253, NJ254, NJ255, NJ256, NJ264, NJ268, PP113, PP114, PP115, PP119, PP122, PP135, PP138, PP139, PP142, PP162, RN282.
Losses Of these 79 aircraft N9048, N9049, P9601, T9071, W3985, W3999, W4004, W4019, W4020, DP177, DP179, DV969 and DV993 were lost due to enemy action. Another 23 were destroyed in accidents; 42 survived.
Catalina/442 Sq. R.C.A.F. W8434.
Catalina/265 Sq. R.A.F. FP300, FP313.
Short C G-AFCZ.
Short G X8233, X8234 and X8275.

SQUADRONS' HISTORIES AT MOUNT BATTEN

R.N.A.S. 1918 Five flights, Nos. 347, 420, 421, 422 and 423 these had added to them Nos. 348 and 349.

R.A.F. 237 Marine Operation Squadron formed from 347, 348 and 349 Flts. in August, 1918. Disbanded 15th May, 1919.

R.A.F. 238 Marine Operations Squadron formed in August 1918 from Nos 420, 421, 422, 423 Flights disbanded April 1922 after being reduced to a Cadre unit.

R.A.F. 203 Squadron formed from 482 Coastal Reconnaissance Flight, using Southamptons, became 203 on the 1st January, 1929. Station Commander Group Captain Busteed departed April.

R.A.F 209 Squadron reformed on the 15th January, 1930. Equipped with *Blackburn Iris* until 1934 when converted to *Perths* up to 1st May, 1935. They left then returned December 1938—December, 1939, with *Stranraers*.

R.A.F. 204 Squadron formed 15 January, 1930 with *Southamptons* then on the 31st August converted to *Scapas*. Undertook a detachment from 23rd September, 1935—August, 1936, when it returned to Plymouth. On the 2nd December, 1937, five *London* IIs left Mount Batten for Australia and they arrived on the 25th January, 1938, returning again on the 29th May. In the July, 1939, 204 converted to *Sunderlands* leaving in April, 1940.

R.Navy 407 Flight. May, 1935, saw the arrival of two flights of aircraft from the Fleet Air Arm Floatplane Base, Lee-on-Solent, commanded by Sqn.Ldr. Salder who at that time was in charge of the catapults. He shortly was promoted to Wing Commander and assumed command of Mount Batten. 407 Fleet Fighter Flight flew *Hawker Ospreys* IIs.

R.Navy 444 Fleet Spotter-Reconnaissance Flight flew *Fairey IIIFs* and was attached to Flight to Capital Ships Home Fleet. With 407 they returned to Lee-on-Solent in November, 1937.

No.2 Anti aircraft co-operation Unit. Flying floatplane *Sharks*, this unit moved to R.A.F. St Eval, wheels being fitted shortly after the War was declared. The work was taken over by 1623 AAC Flt. at Roborough.

No.10 Squadron Royal Australian Air Force Flying *Sunderlands*, formed at Pembroke Dock in Wales, moved to Mount Batten until May, 1941—December, 1941, then back at Pembroke to 31st October, 1945.

No.461 Sq. R.A.A.F. Formed in 1942 on the 25th April. From No. 10 this Squadron moved to Hamworthy in August and then to Pembroke Dock where it had a fine record of War service.

OTHER UNITS

No.934 Balloon Squadron 'W' Flight

No.964 Squadron formed 8th March, 1939, in Plymouth. Became part of 32 Group. In 1940 'W' Flight was formed and in June, 1941, it became part of 934 Balloon Squadron. It was based at Mount Batten and operated nine sites as well as the servicing units at Dartmouth and Plymouth plus a mobile servicing party. Ship-borne balloons were on Naval ships with R.A.F. crews. Flight 'W' was disbanded on the 22 November, 1944.

No.1 Air Despatch and Receipt Unit

Known originally as the *Air Freight Mobile Section* it was formed in June, 1941, although the *Sunderlands* of No. 10 and 204 had been used as a link to the Middle East since before the fall of France in 1940. In April, 1942, it became the No. 1 A.D.R. Unit under Transport Command and closed in April, 1944.

No. 39 Air Sea Rescue Unit, Torquay
Opened in July, 1942, this unit came under Mount Batten in February, 1944, until September of that year. Commenced with one High Speed Launch and controlled by R.A.F. Torquay it was increased to four launches until being handed back.

No. 41 Air Sea Rescue Unit, Salcombe
Opened on the 3rd April, 1942, with two pinnaces it co-operated with the *Walrus* aircraft of 276 Squadron which increased in activity and four HSLs were allocated to the unit. After a fine War record of rescues it was disbanded on the 15th July, 1945, and all equipment and crews transferred back.

No. 43 Air Sea Rescue Unit Mount Batten
Existing from 20th April to 9th September, 1944, it had six HSL on strength which covered the D Day landings.

No. 1101 Marine Craft Unit Fowey
In June, 1942, it was decided to convert a pinnace to target towing and this was sent on detachment to Fowey for two months. This was extended until R.A.F. Fowey was created on the 27th April, 1943, becoming operational on the 28th September of that year. Target towing was the main function and the number of vessels increased to three pinnaces. In April, 1945, the unit was designated No. 1101 MCU and lasted until 5th March, 1958, and transferred to Mount Batten.

Marine Craft known to have been based at one time or another at Mount Batten. HSL 67 foot, 196, 197, 2504, 2515 Ex-Salcombe, HSL 67 foot, 193, 2513 Ex 38ASR/MCU, HSL 67 foot, 2512, 1653, 2655 Ex 48 ASR/MCU, Mk 1A Rescue Target Towing Launches.

PLYMOUTH Roborough Airfield
Requisitioned by the Admiralty in September, 1939, it remained so until June, 1942, when control was taken over by R.A.F. Mount Batten. Units based there included 1623 Anti-Aircraft Co-operation Flight, later 691 Sq., No. 19 Group Communication Flt., Coastal Commands School of Navigation and No. 82 Giding School A.T.C. No. 691 target towing aircraft moved to Harrowbeer airfield in 1945. No. 19 Comm. Flt. remained for many years. The Navigation School closed in July, 1944. Roborough is now a modern airport operated by Brymon Airways.

POSTSCRIPT
A ceremonial disbandment of the Marine Branch took place on the 8th January, 1986, at Mount Batten bringing to an end sixty-eight years of unbroken service. The resident chaplin received a ship's bell as a token of placing the care of the Marine Branch in the hands of the Church. The Service was attended by the Chief of the Air Staff A.C.M., Sir David Craig, and on the 1st February the work of the marine craft was taken over by civilian contractors.

It now seems likely that the closure of the Station, April 1986, is unlikely as the contractors will require facilities to carry out these duties and I have been given to understand the contract is for two years at least, but this information was not from an R.A.F. source. This publication was designed to coincide with the closure, perhaps the happy Station with its cormorant emblem (reputed to have been designed by Lawrence, who else?), will continue for a while longer.

Lowering of the R.A.F. Marine Craft Section Ensign which took place on 8th January, 1986.

LIST OF ILLUSTRATIONS

All author's collection except where credited.

- Cover: Station from the air
  Sunderlands being serviced
- Page 1 Short Sunderland flying boat
- 2 Wg.Cdr. B. Main, M.Mar, E.C.O., R.A.F.
- 3 Station from the Cattewater
- 4 Recommissioning 1918, A. Clamp
  Ferryboat Rapide, A. Clamp
  R.N.A.S. Mess
- 5 Short 184s on Mount Batten pier
  Large America flying boat, Curtiss
- 6 Short 184, S. Walker
- 7 NC.4, Library
  NC.4 outside hangars, Library
- 9 Blackburn Iris being recovered, A. Clamp
  204 Sq. Aircrew
- 10 209 Sq. officers
  209 Sq. other ranks
- 11 Hawker *Osprey* of 407 Fleet Flight, C. Lovelock
  Wapiti on floats about 1931
- 12 Supermarine Southampton
  Blackburn Iris
- 13 Supermarine Southamptons over Plymouth, Library
  Remains of Southampton in Friary Yard, Author
- 14 Fairey IIID
  Scapa Flying boat
- 15 Singapore III, Library
  Singapore III bombing up, Library
- 16 Southampton at Gibraltar, C. Lovelock
  Southampton over Malta, C. Lovelock
  Maintenance, C. Lovelock
  Refuelling, C. Lovelock
  Two pilots, C. Lovelock
- 17 The Tower
- 18 Sunderland of 204 Sq., C. Lovelock
  Crew of Sunderland, C. Lovelock
  French troops, K. Phillips
- 19 Anti-aircraft gun position, Amateur photographer
  Clearing snow, Amateur photographer
- 20 Remains of hangars, R.A.A.F.
  Hangar with tail, R.A.A.F.
  Bomb damage, Amateur photographer
- 21 Plymouth ablaze, Amateur photographer
  A.A. fire, Amateur photographer
- 22 U243 under attack, R.A.A.F.
- 23 U 426 hit and sinking, air crew
- 24 Sunderlands at moorings, Amateur photographer
- 25 Ships in Plymouth Sound for D Day, Amateur photographer
  Sunderland on patrol, Amateur photographer
- 26 Barrage balloon, Amateur photographer
- 27 Servicing engines, Western Morning News
  Working on engine, Amateur photographer
- 28 Pinnace 17, A.R.J. Cowell
  Marine craft, A.R.J. Cowell
- 29 Pinnace 15, A.R.J. Cowell
  Ferryboat, A.R.J. Cowell
- 30 Marine craft, A.R.J. Cowell
  H.S.L.s, A.R.J. Cowell
- 31 119/V in Cattewater, Amateur photographer
  Lost float, Amateur photographer
- 32 Settled, Amateur photographer
  ML839 being salved, Amateur photographer
  ML829 coming up, Amateur photographer
- 33 DD852 on the rocks, Amateur photographer
  Remains on the shore, Amateur photographer
  JM678 on fire, Amateur photographer
- 34 Wall plaque, Amateur photographer
  Cleaning up at Mount Batten, Amateur photographer
  March past 1945, Amateur photographer
- 35 Snap shot, Amateur photographer
  One for the album, Amateur photographer
  On parade outside hangars, Point Cook
  Group photo, Point Cook
- 36 Party
  No. 10 Sq. officers leaving for Australia, Point Cook
- 37 HSL 2513, A.J.R. Cowell
  Dinghy drill, A. Clamp
  Dinghy righting, A. Clamp
- 38 Whirlwind landing
  A.S.R. exercise
  Wessex XV720, V. Fowler
- 39 Commission of HMAFV *Seagull*
  Seal at sea
- 40 Stained glass window, A. Clamp
- 41 Sea Otter H.M.S. *Redpole*
  Beaching cradle
- 42 The Meteorological Office
  Guard House
- 43 R.N.A.S. Cattewater building
  Oldest Station buildings
- 44 Stores
  Wartime gymnasium now store
- 45 Rear of Officers' Mess
  Old Guard House
- 46 General view looking towards the Officers' Mess
  The famous twelve radio masts now reduced to two
- 47 Marine craft No. 1390
  Marine Dock
- 48 Then and Now: The breakwater and barrage balloons
  The deserted breakwater today
  Sunderland off the foreshore
  View of Hoe today
- 49 Then and Now: The Station covered in snow
  Now In the parched conditions of 1984; a British submarine passes
- 50 Wartime shot in front of hangars
  The same hangars today
- 51 The foreshore 1943
  The hangars today which replaced the one destroyed
- 52 1945: A Sunderland over flying the Officers' Mess
  1985: The same view from the tower
- 53 Atlantic serving NATO
- 55 Mount Batten crest
  Lowering of the Marine craft Section ensign, 8th January 1986, R.A.F.

Arthur L. Clamp – the man behind the books

Arthur Leslie Clamp was a man of boundless energy with a passion for helping others, particularly through his love of history. A printer by trade, he started his career in a printing company before moving his family from Exeter to Plymouth to teach at the Plymouth College of Art and Design, where he eventually became the Head of the Printing Department.

A Devoted Family Man

Arthur with his five children.

Despite his love of teaching, Arthur prioritised his family, always making it home by 5:30pm for tea. He and his wife, Rosemary, raised five children: Susan, Angela, Elizabeth, David, and Steven. Arthur would often combine his love of family and history by taking his children on Sunday walks, encouraging them to appreciate historical monuments by taking photos or making crayon rubbings of gravestones for his books. The family home at 203 Elburton Road was a hub of activity, with a large garden, featuring a two-storey fort and a makeshift swimming pool.

A Lifelong Learner and Adventurer

Arthur's thirst for knowledge extended beyond history to a deep curiosity about the world. He was passionate about exploring different cultures, traditions, and cuisines, often taking advantage of his long summer holidays as a teacher to travel to places like India, Russia, South America, the middle east and the USA, sometimes bringing one of his children along. This adventurous spirit even influenced his home life, as seen by the short-lived family tradition of steam-cooking vegetables after a trip to Iceland.

History is a prominent feature of family days out

Community and Philanthropic Spirit

His commitment to serving others was evident in his long-standing involvement with the Elburton Methodist Church. He was the Sunday School Superintendent for over 15 years and served as the editor of the wider church's monthly newsletter, "The Link," for a similar duration. After Rosemary's very sad passing, Arthur later remarried and, following a chance encounter with a professor from India, established a connection with a missionary school in Chennai. Together with his new wife, Christine, he co-founded a "Sponsor a Child's Education" program that continues to this day.

*Pictured left – The cover of 'The Link' complete
with hand drawn sketches of each church by Angela
Below right – Arthur Clamp promoting his latest book
Below left – Arthur at home with his first wife, Rosemary
Below centre – Arthur on holiday with his second wife, Christine*

A Legacy of Learning and Positivity

Arthur's greatest passion was history, which he brought to life through tireless research, documentation, and the many books he authored. He was driven by a need to "never be stuck in a rut," constantly seeking new experiences, meeting new people, and expanding his knowledge. With a positive attitude and a great sense of humour, he was always ready to help others, leaving a lasting impact on his family and community. His children, Susan, Angela, Elizabeth, David, and Steven, remember him with love and gratitude.

David Clamp, 2025

A Legacy of Local History

Below is the story of how Arthur L Clamp began writing books, in his own words, drafted shortly before he passed away in 2001. I have only made minor alterations to this text, correcting grammatical errors that he did not survive to correct himself. When I first discovered this text, I was shocked to see my name mentioned. It seems that, unbeknownst to me, I shared my first PC with him. I suspect he used it during the day when I was at school, although I do have one memory of sitting with him and showing him how it worked. It has been a pleasure to pick up where he left off and see his books republished and redistributed, and to know that I was part of the story, even back then. It was also fascinating to discover that his pricing structure matches the way I have tried to price the books, with a third going to local sellers and the rest covering printing costs with a little left over for my expenses.

I am his eldest grandson, and it is a privilege to curate his legacy, which we are calling 'The Clamp Collection'. The very last line of the text originally reads "The following pages list all the titles." Sadly, that page is missing and we have no record of all the books he published and knowing that some of those were researched by other authors makes the process of finding them even harder. I look forward to one day completing the collection and seeing them all available again. And maybe, one day, I'll even start writing my own to add to the series. For now, here is his story in his own words.

Steven Gibson, 2025

Writing and Publishing Booklets on Local Topics and Areas

I started this interest in either 1968 or 1969 when living in Woodford. I had by these dates established the Department of Printing and I think I must have been looking for something different to do. The first titles were of A5 size proofed from type set at Clarke, Doble and Brendon, Ltd., Plymouth printers, and then made up into pages and printed at Sawtell and Neilson, Ltd., Totnes.

Then began a slow process of getting them out to shops, etc. which proved to be more time consuming and difficult than actually researching, writing and getting the books into print. However, I persisted and opened a business account with Barclays Bank on the Broadway. I was advised to give it a title so I called it "Westway Publications". There came along another problem, one of storage of paper and finished books which was solved when the family moved to Elburton in 1970.

I changed the printer to Penwell, Ltd., Callington, Cornwall, as he was then just setting up himself and his prices seemed very reasonable. I did not get any of the printers to make up the complete books. I hand folded the flat printed sheets, stitched the books on a small manual table stitcher and trimmed them in a small hand turned guillotine which I bought from someone in Penzance for £40. It was brought up in a van.

The trouble and time going to and fro to Callington was too much so I transferred the printing to PDS Printers, Prince Rock, Plymouth, and I have been with them ever since. Now they are at Plympton which is easy to reach and they fold the flat sheets which was turning out to be a long chore which only saved a small part of the printing costs.

All my first titles were written by myself. I took the photographs and developed them in the loft of the house, the type was set by now on a computer situated in the house at Elburton from which I had collected photographic lengths of text to cut up and law down as pages.

At some point I decided that I would do my own film processing of lith film so I bought a large second hand process camera from Kingsbridge and learnt through trial and error to make line negatives of the text and halftone negatives of the illustrations which proved more difficult than I anticipated. The main problem was trying to keep the developer in the large dish at the correct temperature as any change would affect the developing time. I replaced this old camera with a brand new one bought from Croydon, Surrey, costing £900. This has turned out to be a great asset cutting out an expensive part of the printer's costs and one crucial aspect of the work which I could control.

By the middle 1970s there were many outlets I had contacted in Plymouth, up to Dartmoor, Exeter, around to Torbay, Totnes, Dartmouth and the South Hams. The market for local books was much greater than I had first thought and through getting to know many local people undertaking research themselves had the chance to help and make up books for other people who had in most instances, got together a collection of photographs with some text in a rather muddled way. Through my experience in print I was able to shape up their work and get it into print and in every case I had to pay the printer and let the person have the royalties. In the majority of titles produced in this manner this was another way of producing titles and it did give some profit to my work. However, I must say that in a few cases I lost out by either the other person getting the numbers wrong, not returning any monies from stock I delivered or they thought that more of their books should have been sold.

The print run was usually 1,000 copies and from time to time I have had reprints of 250 copies. It took about ten years to clear the first print run so I always had large stocks in the garage, workshop, etc. The numbers sold during the early years was about 7,000 copies a year increasing to around 9,000 copies and for the whole of the enterprise about 500,000 have been sold. The booklets have become part of the local scene and many people collect them, shops regularly order copies and I go around certain areas month by month restocking or replacing titles as necessary.

During the past year or so I have started setting the text on a Packard Bell PC, something which I should have done some years back. I share it with Steven Gibson, my grandson. There appears to be no end to the market for local books, but I could not earn a regular income because of the long time it takes to sell stock.

However, now exceeding 100 titles made up mainly of A4 twenty-four page booklets, some folded guides, with selling prices set with a third going to the shop which is the trade custom, the original idea has been quite successful and could go on for ever.

Apart from monetary benefits, however spasmodically these might be, I have learnt a lot myself, met many interesting people and have become part of the local scene with requests to give talks and to advise people about getting into print.

Arthur L Clamp, 2001

This newspaper article, published by the Evening Herald on 17th August 2001, forms a good record of his life. Just as he encourages us to learn more about local history, we encourage you to learn a little about him. For that reason, we have included these pages at the back of all the most recently republished books, in honour of his memory and recognition of his contribution to the community.

www.ingramcontent.com/pod-product-compliance
Lightning Source LLC
Chambersburg PA
CBHW061401070526
44584CB00031B/4144